# Kenya
## Promised Land?

**above** A game of netball
at Maili 46 Primary
School, Kajiado District

## Geoff Sayer

**facing page**
Turkana girl,
Samburu District

**left to right**
■ Wangui in Uhuru Park,
Nairobi

■ Cattle returning to
their homestead in the
evening, Narok District

**All photographs were taken by Geoff Sayer, unless otherwise indicated**

Published by Oxfam GB
© Oxfam GB 1998
A catalogue record for this publication is available from the British Library

ISBN 0 85598 382 5

Available from the following agents:
*for Canada and the USA:* Humanities Press International, 165 First Avenue, Atlantic Highlands, New Jersey NJ 07716-1289, USA; tel. 732 872 1441; fax 732 872 0717
*for southern Africa:* David Philip Publishers, PO Box 23408, Claremont, Cape Town 7735, South Africa; tel. (021) 64 4136; fax (021) 64 3358
*for Australia:* Bush Books, PO Box 1370, Gosford South, NSW 2250, Australia; tel. (043) 233274; fax: (029) 212248
*for the rest of the world contact:* Oxfam Publishing, 274 Banbury Road, Oxford OX2 7DZ, UK

Published by Oxfam GB, 274 Banbury Road, Oxford OX2 7DZ

Designed by Oxfam CSU JB102/RB/98   Printed by Oxfam Print Unit
Oxfam GB is a registered charity, no. 202918 and is a member of Oxfam International

# Contents

**from top, clockwise**

■ Grandma Koko, Ilkimba, Narok District

■ Snowy summit on the Equator

■ Sunday in Uhuru Park, Nairobi

■ Vehicle-repair workshop at Kamukunji jua kali, Nairobi

# A land of contrasts

Kenya is a land of strong contrasts: a land where mountain summits on the Equator are capped with perennial snow, a land of wide expanses of grasslands and plains, teeming modern cities, palm-fringed beaches, and game parks from which people — except for tourists — have been banished.

There are contrasts too between Kenya's farmers and pastoralists, and their very different ways of life; between modern and traditional values; between the status of landed and landless people; between the values and prospects of young and old; between the lives and aspirations of women and men.

Then there are contrasts between Kenya's rich ruling and commercial elite and the ever-growing numbers of poor and powerless people; between the country's former image as a shining model of economic and political progress, and a far more harsh reality now; between the hopes of those who fought for land and freedom from British rule and the fortunes of those who have lived in Kenya in the years since Independence in 1963.

This book will look at some of those contrasts, and at some aspects of the history of Kenya which continue to shape its present. Above all, it will focus on the lives of modern Kenyans, their hopes and fears, their struggles to improve the quality of their lives, and the many conflicts which lie at the root of the nation, hidden from the sight of the hundreds of thousands of foreign tourists who are attracted by an image of Africa which belies the reality.

**left** Storm clouds promise an end to the dry season, Baragoi, Samburu District

# The Great Rift

**above, top** Looking east across the Rift Valley from Maralal, Samburu District

**above** The shores of Lake Turkana

Kenya's dramatic landscape has been shaped during the last 25 million years by the molten heat of the earth's interior. Up-welling magma lifted and cracked the earth's thin crust to create the highlands of East Africa and Ethiopia, and the deep scars of the Rift Valley that slash through the continent from the Red Sea to Mozambique. Out-pourings of lava along the fault lines of the Rifts threw up volcanoes which include the highest peaks in Africa: Mounts Kilimanjaro and Kenya. Some are still active, as the Rift continues to widen.

The Western Rift forms the modern borders between Uganda, Tanzania, Rwanda, and Burundi on the one side, and their huge neighbour the Democratic Republic of Congo — known until 1997 as Zaire — on the other. It is the Eastern or Great Rift which bisects Kenya, arresting travellers with the views from its rim across ancient savanna grasslands, traversed in distant silhouette by hump-backed Maasai cattle and their herders. In places the scarp falls over 600 metres to the valley bottom, which varies in width from 15 to 90 kilometres.

The Rift is threaded by lakes. The northern-most and largest, with a shoreline twice the length of the Kenyan coast, is Lake Turkana, which boasts Nile perch that can grow to weigh 100kg, and the world's largest population of Nile crocodile. Soda ash thrown out by volcanic eruptions has leached into the lakes farther south. Algae, thriving without competition in the corrosive waters, support one third of the world's population of Lesser Flamingoes. This same ash, forming a hard crust impenetrable to tree roots, has created the vast grasslands of the Maasai Mara and Serengeti.

On the upland plateau west of the Great Rift lies Lake Victoria/Nyanza, source of the Nile, and the world's second-largest freshwater lake. Its waters, rich in fish, are shared by Kenya, Tanzania, and Uganda.

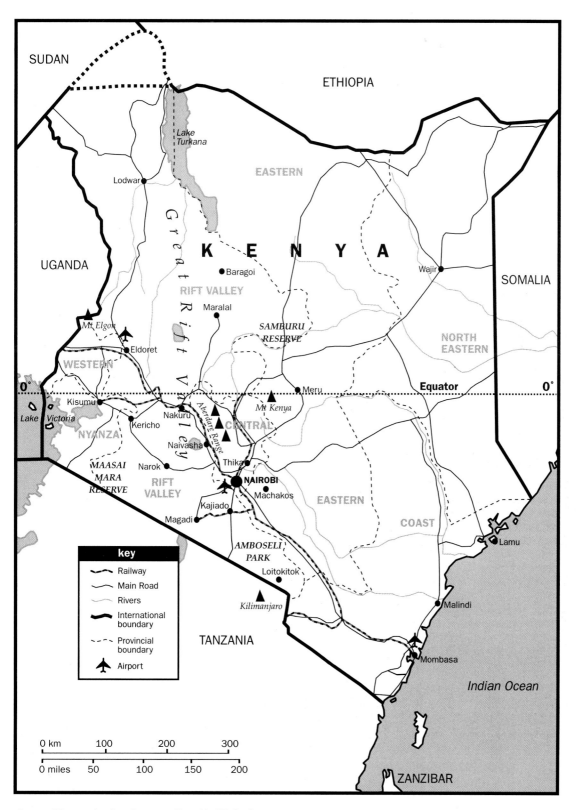

**A map of Kenya, showing places mentioned in this book**

**right** Ome Lokenymeri, dressed in leather tunic and beads. The Turkana people eke a living from the harshest of Kenya's dry northern rangelands.

# The bones
# of our ancestors

Our own flesh and blood began life in eastern Africa, perhaps in what is now Kenya, in the area of woodland, lakeside, and game-rich savanna which supported predators and scavengers: lion, leopard, hyena, vulture, and man. The climate and geology of the Rift Valley have made it a fossil storehouse: the remains of early humans were covered by a blanket of volcanic ash and sediments weathered from the uplands — to be revealed again by more recent rifting and erosion.

## Hunter-gatherers at the dawn of human history

The fossil record shows the evolution of hunter-gatherer societies from the ape-like australopithecines, and the emergence about 1.5 million years ago of our ancestor, Homo Erectus, as the dominant hominid species. Larger-brained than his forebears, and better equipped for walking and running long distances, Homo Erectus spread through Africa, Europe, and Asia during the following million years.

At Olorgesailie, in the Rift Valley south-west of Nairobi, thousands of stone tools can still be seen scattered on the sandy earth, just as they were left half a million years ago by their makers. The hand-axes, cleavers, and scrapers must have been used for butchering and skinning the animals which Homo Erectus hunted or scavenged. Food remains found at the site included birds, zebras, hogs, elephants, baboons, and hippopotami.

Recent studies of DNA in modern populations seem to show that our own species, Homo Sapiens, evolved from Homo Erectus as little as 200,000 years ago, probably in sub-Saharan Africa. From that origin we have peopled the earth.

## The first farmers

The discovery of bone harpoons shows that the teeming wildlife of the Rift Valley lakes may have played a large part in encouraging hunters to settle after 9000 BC. Domesticated livestock were eventually introduced into East Africa from the north, where farming was already well established. By 3000 BC, cattle, sheep, goats, and camels were being herded along the shores of Lake Turkana and the ancient Lake Chalbi, establishing a pastoral tradition that continues today in these arid lowlands. The first evidence of farming in the highlands of southern Kenya comes after 2000 BC, perhaps a result of migration from deteriorating pastures farther north, as the climate became drier.

## Kenya's Iron Age

After 500 BC, Bantu-speaking peoples moved out from the vast tropical forests of west Africa to settle much of eastern and southern Africa, bringing with them the knowledge and practice of iron-working. This new technology had a dramatic impact. Clearing woodland for agriculture, tilling the soil, working timber for construction, waging war — all became easier with iron tools and weapons.

Not long after the Bantu ventured on to the East African plains, the first Nilotic speakers moved south from Sudan into the highlands west of the Rift Valley. These were probably the ancestors of the Kalenjin peoples who occupy much of the area today. Cattle were central to their economy.

The human settlement of the land that became Kenya was completed by the later arrival of Eastern Cushitic speakers who moved into the north-eastern lowlands with their camel herds.

**below** The Hariri ship (based on an illustration dating from AH 634 [AD 1237]): Arab merchants in their cabins, African slaves on deck

# Waterfront to the world

A Greek merchant from Alexandria, writing in about 50 AD, described a thriving trade with 'the markets of Azania' — East Africa. Already weapons — spears, swords, and axes — were being traded by Arab sea-captains for ivory, rhino-horn, and tortoise-shell.

By the ninth century the focus of trade had moved east to the Persian Gulf. Eastern Africa was exporting ambergris, leopard skins, gold, and mangrove poles for ship-building around the Gulf. Slaves were another commodity, taken to extract the salt at Basra, and to drain the marshes of lower Iraq. (The barbaric sea trade in human lives continued until 1872, when the British finally obliged the Sultan of Zanzibar to close down the market.)

The Arabian traders in their triangular-sailed *dhows* brought more than pottery, beads, and cloth: they brought their Islamic religion and customs. Excavations on Shanga Island, near Lamu, have revealed a timber mosque, later rebuilt in coral; established in about 800 AD, it is the oldest mosque found south of Arabia. The discovery of locally minted coins suggests a ruling Muslim dynasty by the year 900.

## Winds of change

The south-west monsoon blows from June to October. On the East African coast, these winds are deflected to south-easterlies, and would have carried the *dhows* north to Arabia. By December the winds turn about, so that any Arab or Persian sailors and merchants who had not made the return journey would remain in the ports for a few months, repairing vessels, buying supplies, and exchanging sea-farers' tales much like those preserved in the stories of Sinbad. Many must have settled with local Bantu women, setting up trading depots in the flourishing towns, or farming the fertile coastal soils. Swahili culture and language grew from this marriage.

**left** The Indian Ocean, viewed from the ruins of Jumba la Mtwana

**below** *Dhows* on the beach near Malindi. Such boats dominated Indian Ocean trade for more than a thousand years.

Though the name 'Swahili' is derived from the Arabic 'sawahil', meaning 'coasts' or 'shores', the language is Bantu, with loan-words from Arabic and other Indian Ocean sources. It spread quickly as a *lingua franca* among the various Bantu-speaking peoples of the coast, while rulers and merchants probably used Arabic. With the development of trade routes into the interior in the nineteenth century, the Swahili language was carried inland to the Great Lakes and beyond, becoming the common tongue of today's Kenya and Tanzania.

It was during the fourteenth and fifteenth centuries that the Swahili towns of the coast flourished, with the busy sea-borne trade helping to create a common culture, expressed in language, architecture, and dress. Mombasa and Malindi became wealthy ports, and new towns such as Gedi and Jumba la Mtwana were founded and briefly flourished. Then the Portuguese arrived, and changed forever the patterns of coastal trade.

## The coming of the Europeans

Arab control of the eastern Mediterranean and the Red Sea had effectively isolated East Africa from European influence — until 1497, when Vasco da Gama, the Portuguese explorer and navigator, sailed round the Cape into the sheltered waters of the Indian Ocean. This began the process of European expansion which led eventually to the partition and colonisation of eastern Africa, and the creation of a State called Kenya.

By 1510, most of the Swahili towns of the East African coast had been sacked and forced into tribute to the Portuguese. Only Malindi, jealous of its powerful rival, Mombasa, formed a lasting alliance with the Portuguese. Mombasa resisted but was eventually abandoned in 1632. By then new and stronger players, the Dutch and the English, had entered the Indian Ocean, intent on dominating the Far Eastern trade.

The Portuguese left few reminders of their stay in Kenya except for Fort Jesus, which still stands. They introduced maize from the Caribbean and left a handful of loan-words in Kiswahili, including *gereza*, which means 'prison', intriguingly derived from the Portuguese *igreja*, meaning 'church'.

**below**

■ Tourists visiting the former Portuguese stronghold of Fort Jesus

■ Jamia Mosque in Nairobi city centre

**right** A tombstone found on Mombasa island, dated 866 AH (1462 AD). The Arabic inscription invokes God's mercy and protection.

**background**
Samburu District

**below**
■ Western Province

■ Samburu District,
Rift Valley Province

## The modern melting pot

Those who have arrived and settled during
the last 2,000 years are the most dominant
groups in modern Kenya. According to the
much-disputed census of 1989, two-thirds of
the population are Bantu-speakers, of whom
the most numerous are the Kikuyu (21 per cent),
Luhya (14 per cent), and Kamba (11 per cent).

Most other Kenyans are Nilotic speakers.
The Kalenjin group (11 per cent) includes
Kipsigis and Nandi. The group took its collective
name in colonial times from a radio programme
which popularised the term 'Kalenjin'. It means
'I tell you' in the Nilotic tongues to which it is
common. The pastoralist Maasai/Samburu
(2 per cent) and Turkana (1 per cent) are also
Nilotes, but most numerous are the Luo, who
live along the shore of Lake Victoria/Nyanza
(12 per cent).

Cushitic speakers comprise the pastoral
peoples of north-eastern Kenya, including the
Somali, Booran, Rendille, and Gabra. Though
they occupy one third of the country, they make
up less than 3 per cent of the population.

Those classed as Kenyan Asian and Arab
numbered less than half of one per cent of the
population in the 1989 census, but they wield a
very significant commercial power. Only 3,184
Kenyan Europeans were counted, though many
more are temporarily resident.

At Independence in 1963, Kenya's
population was 8.5 million. It had risen to some
32 million by 1997, and is projected to reach
45 million by the year 2010.

**from right, clockwise**

- North-Eastern Province

- Nairobi

- Nairobi

- Samburu District,
Rift Valley Province

# Commerce and conquest

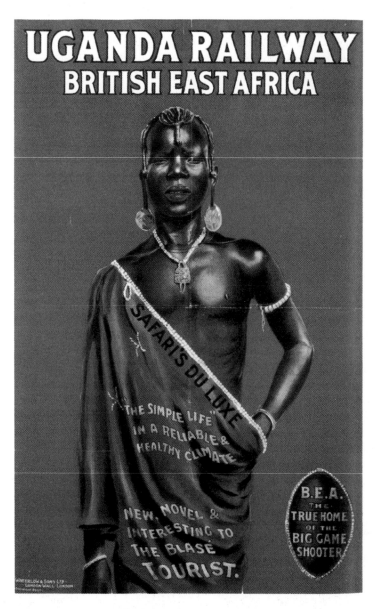

UGANDA RAILWAY
BRITISH EAST AFRICA

SAFARIS DU LUXE

"THE SIMPLE LIFE" IN A RELIABLE & HEALTHY CLIMATE

NEW, NOVEL & INTERESTING TO THE BLASÉ TOURIST.

B.E.A. THE TRUE HOME OF THE BIG GAME SHOOTER

At first, British interest in Kenya was motivated by a desire for free trade rather than by a quest for territorial expansion. The nearby island of Zanzibar was Britain's stepping stone into the East African interior. Exploitation of Kenya's resources proceeded at a brisk pace, overseen by Hindu 'banyans' — financiers and traders from British India. Behind the merchants came the European missionaries — of whom David Livingstone was the most celebrated — intent on saving souls.

## The three C's

Europe's economic greed and technological superiority came to define — and poison — its relationship with Africa. The discovery of quinine in the 1850s helped Europeans to survive malaria, which had previously killed half of the new arrivals within two years. Steamships opened the continent to explorers and adventurers, and gave access to a world market for African commodities: palm oil, rubber, cotton, cocoa, cloves, hides, coconuts, and gum copal (a resin used in varnish). The return trade included assorted hardware, and cloth from Manchester and Bombay. The copper wires of the telegraph revolutionised communications. Above all, the development of weaponry — the breech loader, the repeating rifle, and finally the maxim gun — made even a small European army virtually invincible. Commerce, Christianity, and 'civilisation' were to be imposed by conquest.

## Paper empires

Impelled by European rivalries and fuelled by trade, the partition of Africa became inevitable. By 1900, most of the continent had been parcelled out to the new colonial powers. The Congress of Berlin divided the East African spoils between Britain and Germany. In 1886 a line was drawn from the mouth of the Umba river to Lake Victoria, deviating to the north around Mount Kilimanjaro so that the Kaiser and his aunt, Queen Victoria, could each possess a mountain. The embryonic States of Kenya and Tanzania had been created. (Four years later, the Germans traded Uganda and Zanzibar for the uninhabited North Sea island of Heligoland.) Kenya was declared a British protectorate in 1895.

## The King of the Pink Cheek

Most East Africans knew nothing of these arrangements made in Europe. Almost everywhere in Kenya, British occupation faced popular resistance, which was met by force of arms. Between 1890 and 1907, military expeditions were sent against the Bukusu, the Kamba, the Taita, the Luo, the Ogaden, the Nandi, the Kikuyu, the Embu, the Kipsigis, the Gusii, the Gishu, and the Gabra. Chief Kabongo of the Kikuyu recalled his first visitor from the British administration:

---

*'A Pink Cheek man came one day to our Council. He sat in our midst and he told us of the king of the Pink Cheek, who was a great king and lived in a land over the seas. "This great king is now your king," he said, "and this land is all his land, though he has said you may live on it". This was strange news. For this land was ours. We had no king, we elected our own Councils, and they made our laws. With patience, our leading elders tried to tell this to the Pink Cheek, and he listened. But at the end he said, "This we know, but in spite of this, what I have told you is a fact. ... In the town called Nairobi is a Council or government that acts for the king. And his laws are your laws."'*

---

Relations between the two peoples did not remain civil for long. Francis Hall, who established Fort Hall in the Kikuyu lands in 1899, was proud to claim that natives 'were always shot like dogs when seen'. His successor attacked Muruka on a busy market day. 'Every soul was either shot or bayoneted', he reported. 'Then I went home and wept for a brother officer killed.'

**below** Livingstone's last expedition, 1873

# The Uganda Railway

**UGANDA RAILWAY**
BRITISH EAST AFRICA

STEP BY STEP
THROUGH NATURE'S ZOO

**W**here there were no navigable rivers, railways were seen as the means of opening up Africa. Cecil Rhodes' dream of a route from Cape to Cairo was never realised, but by the late 1890s lines were pushing inland from the coasts of West and Southern Africa. In 1895 the British government decided to build a railway from the Kenyan coast towards Uganda, to ensure control of the interior. A British member of parliament described it as 'a lunatic line to nowhere'.

The line was begun on the mainland opposite Mombasa in 1896. In April 1899 the railhead reached Mile 327, close to the eastern rim of the Rift Valley. 'By this time the only thing that didn't need repair was the foreman's whistle', wrote the Chief Engineer.

A rail camp was set up for repairs and provisions on a marshy plain called by local Maasai herders 'N'erobi' — 'Place of Cold Water'. Succoured by the railway, the settlement, Nairobi, grew rapidly to replace Mombasa as the capital of Kenya (then called the East African Protectorate) in 1907.

After crossing the Rift Valley, the line had to climb through forests to cross Mau Summit at 2,650m. Just before Christmas 1901, the track reached Mile 582 on Lake Victoria, and the first supply train clanked cautiously into Port Florence Station (now Kisumu). A fleet of steamships was already in place to continue the onward journey into Uganda or Tanzania.

The railway's records were well kept. It cost £5,502,592 and 2,498 lives. Almost all these deaths occurred among the 31,983 labourers brought in from India. Most of them returned to India, but 6,724 chose to stay on in East Africa, far outnumbering the few European immigrants. Most became traders, opening *dukas* (shops) and small factories, drawing on the experience of the Indian merchants and middlemen who had long operated on the coast.

In 1902 the eastern province of Uganda became the Kisumu and Naivasha provinces of Kenya, placing the 'Uganda' Railway completely under Kenyan control.

New crops — coffee, tea, and cotton — could now be exported through Mombasa. After 1913, further lines were built from Nairobi, one to Lake Magadi to export soda, and a second to Thika to carry coffee and sisal crops. The overland caravans and the work they provided for the Swahili, Kamba, and Mijikenda were no more.

Already in the nineteenth century railways had revolutionised the social and economic life of the industrialised world. Their impact in East Africa was even more dramatic, stripping away the protection that remoteness had given to the peoples of the interior. Within little more than a generation, their way of life was transformed by this contact with Europeans.

# Kenya Colony

## The White Highlands

The 'Uganda' Railway had to be paid for. How? For Governor Sir Charles Eliot, the answer was clear: bring in white settlers to farm the Highlands, export cash crops and import consumer goods.

Little regard was paid to the rights of Africans by the Europeans who arrived in the early 1900s, greedy for land. A series of labour and land laws entrenched white-settler control at the expense of Africans and Indians. By the early 1930s more than half of the productive agricultural land in Kenya — over 8 million acres — was reserved for little more than 2,000 white farms. Many Africans became squatters and labourers on their own lands, or were confined to 'tribal' reserves. The communities most affected were those which lay in the path of white settlement: the Maasai herders of the plains, the Kikuyu of the eastern highlands, and — to a lesser extent — the Kalenjin, Luo, and Luhya peoples to the west.

The use of forced labour was forbidden in 1921, but hut and poll taxes forced Africans into the cash economy, obliging them to work on the large settler estates. By the early 1920s a quarter of Kikuyus lived as squatters on white farms. African farmers were not allowed to grow tea, coffee, or pyrethrum, which might have given them a means of avoiding paid labour. The hated Kipande was introduced: an identity document which all adult Africans were required to wear in a metal box around their necks. Those with any education were confined to low-grade jobs in the civil service. Brochures aimed at new settlers extolled the virtues of 'Britain's most attractive colony', and generous terms were made available to them. Resources were poured into 'European agriculture', as it was called, but denied to black Kenyan farmers.

## The growth of African nationalism

Even in the 'tribal' reserves, the impact of white settlement on African life and culture was devastating. The local chiefs introduced by the British were alien to most Kenyan peoples. They eventually formed an elite, many using their positions to accumulate land and wealth. As congestion increased and individualism grew, particularly in the Kikuyu lands, traditions of land tenure and inheritance began to break down. Men were forced to leave their families to look for work. Migration to the towns created squatter settlements like Pangani in Nairobi, where the seeds of a new African nationalism germinated among Kenyans who had gleaned an education from the missionaries. Their grievances were heightened by the bitter experience of Kenyans in the First World War. Though only 10,000 fought in the campaign against the Germans in Tanganyika, more than 160,000 were recruited, often forcibly, as porters. A quarter of them perished.

The colony's Legislative Council admitted Indians in 1923, but no African was appointed until 1944. The political power of the settlers grew steadily, and there were even occasional threats to kidnap the Governor or to issue unilateral declarations of independence from Britain. An ironic result of all this huffing and puffing was that Kenyan politicians learned the power of civil disobedience and protest. Among them was one Jomo Kenyatta.

Kenyatta — born Kamau wa Ngengi — received his schooling at a Church of Scotland Mission. Moving to Nairobi, he took jobs as a court interpreter and meter reader, and became active in the African political organisations which emerged in the 1920s. By 1928 he had become General Secretary of the Kikuyu Central Association, which took the land issue as the focus of its struggle. In 1929 and again in 1931 he was sent to London to campaign for the nationalist cause, staying on in Europe until 1946. He studied first at Moscow University and then at the London School of Economics, and was active in helping to establish the Pan-African Movement.

When Kenyatta returned, it was to an even more volatile situation. All political parties had been banned for the duration of the Second World War, and many leaders were imprisoned. Forced labour had been introduced on tea and coffee plantations. Unrest simmered as squatters were pushed off white farms, urban unemployment increased, and the cost of living rose. In 1947, Kenyatta was elected President of the Kenya African Union (KAU), which had been formed in 1944 and was demanding greater political and economic advancement for Africans.

The war had given new skills and a new awareness to many Kenyans. Over 90,000 had been recruited into the armed forces, seeing active duty in Burma, Madagascar, and Ethiopia. Some had served in India, where they learned of the Indian movement for independence. Some, like trade unionist Bildad Kaggia, met black American officers. Above all they learned, in Kaggia's words, that 'Africans, given education and opportunity, were capable of doing everything that the *mzungu* (white man) could do'. Demobilised, these men — cooks, carpenters,

engineers, truck drivers — could find no work. This was the recruiting ground for KAU and Mau Mau.

## The struggle for independence

KAU became the mouthpiece of African nationalism in Kenya, and a forum for vigorous debate between moderates and radicals. With the involvement of the increasingly powerful trade union movement, KAU's membership grew to about 100,000 by 1952. It was dominated by the Kikuyu, because they were affected most acutely by the problem of landlessness and land alienation, and made up two thirds of the population of Nairobi. But their objective was Kenyan, not Kikuyu, independence.

Speaking to mass rallies throughout the country, Kenyatta continued to urge non-violence. But radicals in KAU had despaired of peaceful change, launching an underground movement to overthrow the ruling minority. To achieve unity and commitment, the members adopted the use of oaths, a practice which united the Kikuyu as nothing else could have done; unfortunately it largely excluded non-Kikuyu.

Arson, cattle-maiming, and the killing of 'loyalists' provoked increasing hysteria among the settlers. In October 1952 the Governor bowed to pressure and declared a State of Emergency which was to last until January 1960. The Mau Mau rebellion had begun.

## Mau Mau

The refusal of the British to respond to demands for political rights had fuelled nationalist resistance. As the nationalists took up arms, the government rounded up their leaders, including the moderates who might have mediated for peace. Jomo Kenyatta and nearly 100 others were imprisoned, following trials which were travesties of justice. A few months later, KAU was banned. The government established police posts throughout the Kikuyu Reserve and armed a 'loyalist' Homeguard. All squatters had to be photographed, but many refused. About 100,000 were evicted by the end of 1953.

The government's crackdown only drove more disaffected Kenyans into the forests of Mount Kenya and the Aberdares, where General China and Dedan Kimathi had established the

Land and Freedom Army — or Mau Mau, as it came to be known. Their war was waged as much against collaborators — police, civil servants, chiefs, landowners — as it was against the European settlers. Inevitably it was the Kikuyu who suffered most during the years of bitter conflict which ended with Kimathi's capture in October 1956.

During Operation Anvil in 1954, Nairobi was combed by 25,000 soldiers attempting to flush out the Mau Mau supporters who were supplying arms and food to the fighters. About 20,000 were sent to reserves, and another 30,000 to detention camps. On the reserves, one million Kikuyu and Embu were forced to relocate into 'protected' villages. Land was confiscated and awarded to 'loyalists'. In Operation Hammer, launched in 1955, the British began bombing the forests, and hunted Mau Mau with gangs of surrendered guerrillas who knew their mountain hideouts.

Though government statistics underestimate the loss of African lives, they are stark evidence of the balance of power, and of death, in the first four years of the Emergency. Over 13,000 African fighters and civilians were killed, and over 1,000 hanged. Thirty-two White and 26 Asian civilians were killed. The security forces lost 167 dead, more than half of them Africans.

## Uhuru — 'Freedom'

The Crown Colony's dependence on British troops confirmed that Kenya could not be a White Man's Country like Rhodesia. Even as the fighters were pushed higher into the Aberdares, the government began gradually to concede greater power to the nationalists. In 1954 one African minister was nominated to the Legislative Council. Three years later, Africans were elected to the Council for the first time, giving the eight successful candidates, led by Tom Mboya and Oginga Odinga, a new legitimacy. Among the eight was a future President, Daniel arap Moi.

By 1960 there were 14 African members, and all flew to the first of the two Lancaster House conferences held in London to chart a course towards African rule. Following elections in May 1963, Kenyatta became Prime Minister. On 12 December he led his country to independence.

As recently as 1960 the British governor had described Kenyatta as 'an African leader to darkness and death'. Kenyatta, however, turned the other cheek to his former oppressors and preached the need for reconciliation. A collection of his speeches, published in Kenya in 1968, was entitled *Suffering Without Bitterness*.

**above** Crowds welcome Jomo Kenyatta after his release from detention, 14 August 1961

Ian Berry/Magnum

# Independence and after

**M**easured against most of its neighbours — Somalia, Ethiopia, Sudan, Uganda, Congo, Rwanda — Kenya has enjoyed stability and relative peace since Independence. Elections have been held regularly, and there has never been a military government. Jomo Kenyatta, the first Kenyan President, died in his bed in 1978 and was succeeded peacefully and constitutionally by his Vice-President, Daniel arap Moi, who has been in power ever since. Despite conflict and realignments within the ruling Kenya African National Union (KANU), the centre has held firm. The benefits of such stability should not be underestimated: most signally they include the roads, schools, and water-supply systems which were built during the first two decades after Independence.

Until the 1990s, Kenya was regarded very positively by the West. Its relative stability in an unstable region, its pro-Western policies, its acceptance of Western military bases, its land-reform programme — hailed as a model by the World Bank — and the experiences of literally millions of foreign tourists on its beaches and in its game parks have all contributed to this. But recent years have seen a gradual change, and this image has become increasingly tarnished. How has this happened?

## A fragmented nation

One damaging legacy of colonialism in Kenya is the fragmented nature of civil society. During the Mau Mau years, in order to isolate the Kikuyu, the British administration refused to allow political parties to operate at a national level. So parties were formed locally, and mobilised their support locally. The prohibition helped to shape a political system which is fragmented along ethnic fault lines. The opposition to KANU, the ruling party, is fatally divided, and KANU's grip on power seems to be unassailable.

## The rise and rise of KANU

Formed in 1960 by Tom Mboya, Oginga Odinga, and James Gichuru, KANU drew its main support from the Kikuyu and Luo. The

Kenya African Democratic Union (KADU), established a few months later under the leadership of Ronald Ngala, was supported mostly by the coastal peoples, by the pastoral Maasai and Kalenjin, and also by some settlers. One of its leaders was Daniel arap Moi, a member of the Kalenjin group. While KANU pushed for a strong central government, KADU, fearing domination by the more numerous Kikuyu and Luo, favoured a federal structure with powers devolved to the regions. This set the pattern for the politics of Kenya to the present day.

After losing the elections of 1961 and 1963, KADU dissolved itself, and most of its members, including Moi, joined KANU. In 1966 Oginga Odinga, formerly Vice-President, created the Kenya Socialist People's Union. This was banned in 1969 following killings in the wake of Tom Mboya's assassination. Kenya then became a *de facto* one-party State.

The arguments in favour of a one-party system stressed the need for stability and nation-building. The main argument against it was that any expression of dissent, by trade unions or students or women's groups, for example, was seen as treachery. In the 1990s, supporters of constitutional reform argued that the time had come for Kenya to move into a more mature phase, in which those in power should no longer criminalise political debate.

## Multi-partyism — but is it democracy?

Following the demise of the Soviet Union, Kenya's strong anti-communist stance was no longer a guarantee of favours from Western donors. In November 1991, they suspended aid to Kenya until President Moi lifted the ban on opposition parties. This he promptly did. Of the parties which subsequently emerged, the strongest threat seemed to be presented by FORD, the Forum for the Restoration of Democracy, which brought together leading Luo and Kikuyu politicians, including the veteran Odinga. FORD attracted some grassroots support, but in August 1992 it split between the Luo Odinga, who formed FORD-Kenya, and the Kikuyu Kenneth Matiba, who formed FORD-Asili. The Kikuyu vote was further split by the rivalry between Matiba and Mwai Kibaki, who had established the Democratic Party.

Taking advantage of these splits, and in a context of increasing ethnic violence which was blamed by many observers on the government, Moi called a snap election. The government held all the levers of power and was able to print money to ease KANU through the campaign. KANU won 112 of the 200 seats in the National Assembly, with only 35 per cent of the vote, and Moi was returned as President.

Had the Opposition leaders been able to sublimate their individual lust for power, to put the country's interests first and unite behind a single candidate, the result would perhaps have been different.

## Divide and rule: the politics of ethnicity

The use and abuse of ethnicity has a long history in Kenya. In colonial times, political activity was restricted to the local rather than the national level, and this tendency continued after Independence. Under Kenyatta, it was the Kikuyu (and to a lesser extent the Luo) who dominated. Under Moi it has been the Kalenjin, and to a lesser extent the Kamba, Maasai, and Kisii. Kalenjin now dominate the civil service, and government investment favours the home areas of the Kalenjin and their allies. 'Divide and rule' was the British motto, and Kenyan rulers learned the lesson well. Moi has encouraged a kind of political apartheid in which 'KANU zones' have been created in the countryside, by the eviction of communities suspected of disloyalty, and by the award of their land to KANU supporters. The short-term result has been Moi's own political survival, but in the longer term the prospects for civil strife and instability are likely to increase.

## The poverty gap becomes a rift

Despite the social and economic progress made after Independence, the rich in Kenya have become steadily richer, while the poor are increasingly impoverished. J. M. Kariuki, a former Mau Mau detainee who was assassinated in 1975, expressed it aptly when he warned: 'We do not want a Kenya of ten millionaires and ten million beggars.' But Kenyatta, through his own accumulation of wealth, encouraged acquisitive tendencies among his entourage. Concentration of economic and political power in the office of the President has continued — and

indeed intensified — under President Moi, giving rise to the joke *L'état c'est Moi*.

Western companies have always been welcomed in Kenya, not least because their presence allowed the local *Wabenzi* (owners of Mercedes Benz cars) to grow rich on the bribes they could extract for offering 'security'. The *Wabenzi* were also able to use their positions to acquire land, often at ridiculously low prices, for speculation. Corruption, nepotism, and smuggling have come to permeate the whole system of government, the civil service, and the police. (A new supermarket in a suburb of Nairobi was reported in 1997 to be unable at the last minute to open for trading, because a close associate of a government minister suddenly announced that he had been given title to the verge between the supermarket entrance and the road, and he was demanding £500,000 in return for access.) Everything has a price, from a major international contract to the *kitu kidogo*, a 'little something', that must be handed over for a driving licence or new ID card, or to escape police custody for a fictitious motoring offence. Even some of Kenya's banks have been rocked by allegations of corruption, and top government officials and leading politicians have been implicated in the notorious 'Goldenberg scandal', a fraud involving fictitious exports of gold and diamonds, which has cost Kenya's treasury nearly US$500 million.

In its Poverty Assessment Report (1995), the World Bank estimated that 46 per cent of Kenya's rural population and 30 per cent of the urban population were living below the poverty line in 1992. The poor in Kenya are becoming poorer. The country's resources have become increasingly concentrated in the hands of a few, with 10 per cent of the population holding 48 per cent of the wealth.

There is nothing inevitable about these statistics. Processes at work in society and the economy bring wealth to some, while others are reduced from vulnerability to destitution.

Nairobi: Riverside Park (above) and Mathare Valley (below) — same city, worlds apart

# Kenya at the crossroads

**M**odern Kenya has not been a tolerant society. Detention without trial is common. There has been a long, violent history of confrontation between the authorities and students and academics. There is little faith in the judicial system, which is heavily weighted in favour of the rich and powerful. People have no protection against violence by the police. As a result, they often take the law into their own hands, and mob justice ensues.

By 1997, the world could no longer ignore the violence which had become endemic in Kenyan society. Demonstrations by students and others calling for political reform were brutally dispersed by the police; even the sanctuary of the churches was not respected. Televised scenes of armed police crashing into Nairobi's Anglican Cathedral, tear-gassing the congregation and clubbing defenceless clergy, provoked a major political and economic crisis.

Widespread international criticism of political brutality and financial corruption led the International Monetary Fund in an unprecedented move to suspend further aid to Kenya: a package of soft loans worth US$220 million, negotiated under the Enhanced Structural Adjustment Facility (ESAF), would not be implemented until steps were taken to stamp out corruption and mismanagement. In response, the value of the Kenya shilling fell to an all-time low, new investment all but dried up, and aid from Japan and Germany, Kenya's biggest donors, seemed threatened.

## Ethics or ethnicity?

Despite the problems crowding in on him — the loss of international confidence, rampant corruption, crumbling roads and communications, the worst cholera outbreak in a decade — Mr Moi and his party, KANU, won the presidential and legislative elections in December 1997. In 1992, he had stood against seven candidates.

In the 1997 election, he was challenged by 14. The lessons of 1992 had not been heeded. The opposition political parties remained divided and highly antagonistic to each other. They lacked any serious alternative economic and social policies, and were out of touch with people at the grassroots. Most leaders, it was widely believed, simply sought power to exploit it for their own profit.

Kenya is a very young nation, and multi-partyism less than a decade old. As more and more Kenyans begin to argue for a new morality in public life, will the next generation of politicians be guided by ethics, rather than ethnicity? One sign of hope is that the emerging middle classes are becoming more outspoken in their demands for political and

**above** Leonard on duty in Chiromo, Nairobi: rising crime rates generate jobs in the security industry

constitutional reform. Among them is a small group of constitutionalists, mostly lawyers and church-people, who are often not members of any political party. By their persistence they have brought the whole question of civil and political liberties into the public arena, spreading their message throughout the country through their church-based networks.

President Moi has gone some way to meet the demands of the constitutionalists. Censorship of playwrights and film-makers, for example, has ended, and it is now possible to hold a public meeting without an official permit. Press freedom, once greatly circumscribed, is growing; the boundaries are being tested and extended by the Aga Khan's Nation Group in *The East African* and *The Daily Nation*, and by Opposition leader Kenneth Matiba in *The People*. They now break stories that others, fearful of the unwritten rules of censorship, would not dare to touch. But the reformists want more fundamental change: the rooting out of corruption, a more equitable land-tenure system, and reform of local government.

The scarcity of political alternatives is deeply worrying in a country where ethnicity has become a potentially explosive factor. Local politicians now openly demand that 'their' people should not be governed by 'foreigners' (fellow Kenyans from different tribes), in a manner which would be inconceivable in either Tanzania or Uganda.

For the Labour government elected in the United Kingdom in 1997, Kenya poses particularly difficult problems. In the past, Britain's criticisms of Kenya have been muted, not least because of the huge amount of British investment in the country. But for many British policy makers, Moi is now seen as one of the dinosaurs of Africa. Everyone is conscious of the fate of ex-President Mobutu of Zaire, and questions are being asked: has the time come for British policy towards Kenya to be realigned?

# Tea & tourism – coffee & carnations

Kenya's economy has long been dominated by agriculture. It accounts for almost 30 per cent of the nation's Gross Domestic Product and generates about 60 per cent of the country's foreign-exchange earnings. Although 80 per cent of Kenya's land surface is classified as arid or semi-arid, the agricultural sector is strikingly diversified.

Tea overtook coffee as an export earner in 1989, and by the late 1990s Kenya was competing with Sri Lanka to become the largest exporter in the world. Tea now brings in about one-quarter of Kenya's total foreign exchange, and employs more than one million people, directly or indirectly. The leaves are picked by hand, all the year round. One-third of Kenya's high-quality tea is exported to Britain. Coffee is the third-most important hard-currency earner, after tea and tourism, but production is vulnerable to drought and disease. Just behind it comes commercial horticulture, which has enjoyed a spectacular rise, exporting off-season fresh fruits (strawberries, pears, and pineapples), vegetables (avocado and mange-tout), and cut flowers (carnations) to the European market.

Industry and manufacturing make as yet a smaller contribution to the economy, but Kenya has declared its intention to become an industrialised nation by 2020. Tourism is a major source of foreign currency, though numbers of visitors have declined in recent years. Desperate searches for oil have so far yielded nothing, and oil imports consume more than one-third of the value of Kenya's export earnings.

## A place in the global economy ...

Independent Kenya adopted a pro-Western stance in the economic sphere as well as the political sphere. Unlike neighbouring Tanzania, it opened its doors wide to Western investors, provided that they had local 'supporters'.

**above** Margaret Wanjiru picking coffee on the family *shamba* near Murang'a, Central Province

Nationalisation and State ownership were not embraced, despite a certain amount of early rhetoric about African socialism. Over the years the influence of foreign investors and multinational corporations such as Lonrho and Unilever has steadily increased. The UK is the biggest investor in Kenya, with an investment portfolio of more than US$1.5 billion in a wide range of enterprises. Tax incentives are generous, and repatriation of profits and royalties has gone unchecked. The emphasis has been on growth, rather than distribution. By international standards, Kenya has not incurred a huge debt: its borrowings have been stable at around $7bn since 1990. (In human terms, however, this means that every Kenyan citizen inherits a debt of some $3,200 at birth.)

In many ways Kenya was better prepared than other countries for the era of economic structural adjustment which began in the mid-1980s. This entailed a switch from the early policy of import-substitution, under which Kenya aimed to produce its own goods, such as drinks and tobacco, textiles, food, and electrical and paper products; instead, Kenya adopted a policy of liberalisation, which was intended to reduce the direct involvement of the government in the economy, for example by ending price controls on imported goods and dismantling monopoly marketing boards. In reality, competition (on which liberalisation was based) is poorly developed, and attempts to privatise key parastatal organisations have run into fierce opposition from the politically powerful who have vested interests to safeguard.

### ... and prospects for the regional economy

Recently there have been serious attempts to reactivate the East African Community, established after Independence. It collapsed in 1977 in a welter of mutual recriminations between Kenya, Uganda, and Tanzania. A Tripartite Commission for East Africa was launched in February 1996 with relatively modest ambitions, seeking initially to improve links in transport, energy, fishing, and cross-border trade. There seem to be good prospects for greater regional economic cooperation, which could extend to include Somalia and Ethiopia. Already, Uganda and Tanzania have overtaken Britain as the largest export markets for Kenyan products.

### Kenya's dual economy

Like many countries in Africa, Kenya has a dual economy, marked by a wide gulf between its modern and traditional sectors.

The modern economy is primarily urban and cash-based, and is linked to national and international market systems. It includes people who are engaged in waged employment, and the vast numbers who operate in the 'informal sector' — the unregulated sphere where goods and services are traded on a small scale.

By contrast, the traditional system, which includes over half of Kenya's population, is poorly integrated, if at all, into the modern cash economy. It is designed principally to meet the needs of the household economy and is primarily run by women. People farm the land in order to feed themselves and to sell any surplus crops for cash to pay for essentials like clothing, school fees, and medical expenses. They use family labour and occasionally hire extra help. They carry on sowing, planting, harvesting, and herding year after year. Access to land is absolutely crucial to their survival.

This system exists quite separately from the modern one. Though men working in towns do send money back to their families in rural areas, they tend to do so only in emergencies. They also tend, over time, to establish new families in the towns, so that increasingly households in rural areas are headed by women. The modern economy is not central to the survival of rural households, and debates about economic development policy are scarcely relevant to the daily lives of those who toil in the traditional sector.

## Kenya's Gross Domestic Product

**Agriculture:** 30 per cent
**Tourism:** 19 per cent
**Manufacturing:** 10 per cent
**Livestock production:** 10 per cent

**Annual total for 1996:** US$9 billion

### Value of main exports (1996) in US$ million

**Tea:** 397
**Coffee:** 288
**Horticultural products:** 239
**Petroleum products (re-exports):** 123
**Cement:** 45
**Pyrethrum extract:** 28

**Exports:** to Uganda 16 per cent,
Tanzania 13 per cent, UK 10 per cent,
Germany 8 per cent

**Imports:** from UK 13 per cent, South Africa,
Germany, United Arab Emirates, and USA
7 per cent each

# Smallholders and agribusiness

**M**ost of Kenya's agricultural and cash-crop production is confined to the coastal belt and the Central and Western Highlands, using less than one-fifth of the country's land surface and supporting more than three-quarters of its population.

Away from these areas of higher rainfall, conditions become more and more marginal for agriculture. Farmers may risk growing maize and succeed in a good year, but the indigenous African dryland cereals, sorghum and millet, are more reliable, supplemented by cow peas and pigeon peas.

The surrounding grasslands and bushlands, where rainfall is too low to sustain regular cultivation, are home to the pastoralist peoples who depend for their livelihood on cows, sheep, goats, and camels.

## The Central Highlands

The road north from Nairobi reveals a cross-section of the contrasting uses of Kenya's fertile highlands. It descends gently through Thika, past thousands of hectares of Del Monte pineapples and huge, privately owned coffee and sisal estates. Passing through Murang'a, formerly the frontier garrison of Fort Hall, the road rises quickly through a patchwork of crops and ferny Grevillea trees. The terraced red earth seems permanently clothed with beans and maize, bananas and coffee bushes, sweet potatoes and 'Irish' potatoes, and Napier grass grown as fodder for stall-fed cows. On some of the shambas coffee has become conspicuous by its absence, the effect of falling world prices after 1988. Farmers have to remove the bushes surreptitiously, for the law forbids it.

As the land continues to rise, tea takes over as the preferred cash-crop, thriving in the moist, acidic soils above 1,600m. Whole hillsides are given over to the neat privet-like hedges. Tea farmers seem happy enough with their crop, selling it to buy vegetables from their neighbours and maize meal from the local trading centre. By the late 1990s, smallholders were growing well over half of Kenya's tea.

Two generations ago, Mau Mau resistance fighters hid in thick bush among these hills. Now, from valley to valley, every inch is in use. Beans and sweet potatoes reach out across the drainage gullies lining the earth roads,

**right** Murang'a District, Central Province: Peter Thuo and his mother, Margaret Wanchiro, collecting fodder for their stall-fed cow

**below** Gaudencia and Anthony Obon'go picking kale on their organic smallholding in Koguta, Kisumu District, Nyanza Province. Organic farming is labour-intensive but highly productive, and requires no costly inputs.

threatening to reclaim them from the lorries that wind their way up to collect the tea and coffee harvests.

## The smallholder revolution

In the early days of self-government, when the energies of Kenya's smallholder farmers were unleashed, the country enjoyed remarkable economic growth. The Million Acre Scheme of the early 1960s settled 34,000 families on prime farmland previously set aside for Europeans. A further 100,000 hectares were redistributed between 1971 and 1976.

Under British rule, Africans had been forbidden or discouraged from growing coffee, tea, and pyrethrum, which were the settlers' crops, grown on large estates. But by the early 1980s, smallholders were producing over 60 per cent of Kenya's coffee and almost 40 per cent of its tea. More importantly, they were producing most of the country's staple food, maize, which supplies almost half of the nation's calories and more than one-third of its protein. Though often bought and eaten roasted on the cob at the roadside, most is ground to flour — *posho* — and boiled in water to make *ugali*, a solid porridge eaten with the fingers, or *uji*, a thinner gruel.

Kenya has been more or less self-sufficient in food for more than 30 years, and today Kenya's three million smallholdings account for over 70 per cent of agricultural production and over 85 per cent of agricultural employment, on less than half of the cultivable land.

## Agribusiness — from horizon to horizon

Despite the programme of land-redistribution, many large farms, ranches, and plantations remained under European control after Independence. Others were bought by the Kenyan political and business elite. Though reliable figures are not available, it seems that more than one-third of the best agricultural land is still owned by fewer than 1,000 families and companies.

Some of these enterprises provide products which are household names in the UK, Kenya's biggest export market for foods and beverages. Brooke Bond, owned by Unilever, manages tea estates that roll from horizon to horizon around the town of Kericho.

**above**
Del Monte pineapple plantation near Thika, Central Province

Del Monte tend an extensive pineapple mono-culture, most of it for canning or juicing. Kenya boasts the world's most extensive carnation farm, and in 1996 overtook Israel to become the leading supplier of cut flowers to the Dutch auctions.

But big is often not beautiful in African agriculture. Most of Kenya's large holdings grow maize and wheat, or graze cattle for beef and dairy products. These are highly mechanised farms which employ little labour — Kenya's most abundant commodity. Studies have shown that mechanised maize farms require 11 days of unskilled labour per hectare per year, while the comparable figure for a smallholding is over 30 days. In dairy production the contrast is even greater: no unskilled labour is used on the large open-grazed farms in Nakuru, while a smallholding is reckoned to require 35 days per hectare per year.

Yet the large farms are not cost-efficient. A World Bank assessment in 1994 concluded that 'the efficiency of many large-scale operations is low: wheat farms and open-grazing dairying operations in particular are very inefficient ... and are highly protected by subsidised credit and import tax advantages'. Tax exemptions highlight the favoured treatment of the large-scale farmer. Tractors, combine harvesters, and mechanised plough-ing equipment are exempt from import duties and VAT; whereas spades, hoes, wheelbarrows, handcarts, and manual or animal-drawn ploughs have attracted import duties as high as 70 per cent, as well as VAT at between 5 and 18 per cent.

There is some evidence that large holdings are gradually being divided and reduced in size. An equalisation of taxes and benefits might accelerate this change and increase agricultural production and employment. But the powerful interests vested in land-ownership are unlikely to yield easily to demands for further redistribution of land to small-scale farmers.

### The limits to growth

It was pressure on the land that arrested the rapid growth of Kenyan agriculture in the 1980s and 1990s, when the annual increase in output slowed from almost five per cent to under one per cent per year, well below the growth in population. Most worrying are recent falls in maize production, which have undermined Kenya's self-sufficiency in food.

As land has been sub-divided within families, plots have become smaller. More than half of all smallholdings measure less than one hectare. Increasing numbers of farmers have moved on to drier lands previously used for grazing, while the poorest rural dwellers, with little or no land, depend on wage labour. Many have moved to the towns, with no option but to join the growing numbers of squatters living in shanties and slums.

### A success story from Machakos

Dry-land farming can be made sustainable, and the proof is to be found in the semi-arid, drought-prone Machakos District, just south of Nairobi. It is one of the most remarkable agricultural success stories in the whole of Africa: long-term studies have shown that, in an area regarded by the British as eroded, degraded, and overpopulated, local people have adapted dynamically to harsh conditions and population growth, and the condition of the natural environment has recovered almost entirely.

The Kamba people who live in Machakos traditionally depended more on livestock than on agriculture. With the creation of the Ukamba Reserve in 1906, they were hemmed in by settler ranches and Crown Lands, which increased the pressure on their grazing lands. By the 1930s, Machakos was reported to be 'a parching desert of rocks, stones, and sand'.

Today the density of population in Machakos is three times what it was in 1930, yet erosion of the soil is negligible. The hillsides bear witness to the transformation: thousands of kilometres of neatly tiered terraces have restored the soils and increased the potential for cultivation. The terraces are created by throwing soil up-hill to form a bank, which can reach 2 metres in height. Much of this arduous work has been carried out by self-help groups. Organised mainly by women, they were built on Kamba traditions of *mwethya* and *mwilaso*, in which friends, neighbours, and relatives come together to work on each other's farms.

A quarter of the land is now under crops, compared with just one-tenth in 1930. Maize and beans predominate, but coffee and vegetables are also important cash-earners, and exotic fruit trees thrive. Cattle numbers are much as they were in the past, with an increasing proportion of cross-bred cattle which are stall-fed on crop residues and fodder crops. Known to Kenyans as 'grade' cows, they produce much more milk than the zebu cattle which are so well adapted for survival on dry rangelands. Their manure serves as a fertiliser for the crop land.

Since 1930 the value of output per person in the Machakos District has increased threefold, while output per hectare has increased tenfold. This success challenges much received wisdom about African agriculture.

## The coast

Hot and humid, with rainfall throughout most of the year, the coast feels and looks quite different from the rest of Kenya. Its farmers and fishers are Mijikenda — Bantu peoples with a mix of Arab ancestry. Most numerous among the Mijikenda are the Digo and Giriama.

The landscape is distinguished by its elegant stands of coconut palm, which seem everywhere to be at the heart of the rural economy. The leaves are used as *makouti*, the coast's roofing thatch, and for making large baskets often used for carrying the mango crop. Copra, the white fleshy interior of the nut, provides oil for cooking and soap-making. Mats, rope, and upholstery filling are made from coir — the fibres filling the outer husks of the coconut. Combs, buttons, and cups can be made from the shell itself, though the production of souvenir novelties for the tourist trade has become a more profitable business. But the tree's most important product is palm wine, a speciality of the Giriama people, which is traded along the length of the coast. Mangoes, oranges, and cashews are also grown as cash crops, and maize, rice, and tropical vegetables for food.

**above** Adabu Simon and Rukia harvesting maize on the coast

# Pastoralism or 'progress'?

**M**ore than half of Kenya is classified as arid land, receiving less than 400mm of rainfall in an average year. Here livelihoods depend mainly on livestock, and the key to survival is mobility. Herders and their cattle, sheep, goats, and camels follow the rains and the best grazing through the seasons, their way of life adapted to the ecology of the dry lowland plains. Milk is the staple food.

In and around the Rift Valley live the pastoralist peoples of the Maasai, Samburu, Pokot, and Turkana; in the north and east live the Somali, Booran, Gabra, and Rendille. The relationship between people, animals, and land has evolved over thousands of years, since the first domesticated stock reached Lake Turkana before 2000 BC.

A five-year-old Maasai boy can identify a dozen species of acacia bush that all look much the same to the visitor, and can explain their different uses. He may be trusted to tend goats close to the homestead, and will play with small stones which are his 'cattle', taking them out to graze and bringing them back to the safety of their *boma* in the evening. His way of life has been moulded to exploit an unpredictable environment to the full.

## The myth of overgrazing

In Maa — the Maasai language — you cannot say, 'I own this land' — only 'I use this land'. For thousands of years the rangelands belonged to no one — or to everyone. But farming societies based on private tenure of land have always viewed communal land-ownership with prejudice. Because livestock are owned by individuals, and grazed on communal land, it was assumed that over-grazing and degradation of vegetation would be the inevitable result. It was assumed that

**right** Simon tending cattle outside his homestead at Iltilal, Kajiado District, Rift Valley Province

individuals competing for grazing resources would have no short-term incentive to conserve them.

This reasoning, known as 'the tragedy of the commons', has more recently been rejected by researchers working in Africa's arid lands. They argue that in the unstable dryland environment, where rainfall is unpredictable, both from year to year and in its geographical distribution each year, herds have to keep moving in search of food and water. Inevitably there are years in which drought affects an entire region and plant growth is prevented. At these times, animals will die or be sold, usually at very low prices. The most skilful herders will survive the drought; the less skilful may be reduced to destitution.

When good rains return, the drought-hardy plant-life recovers quickly, and is likely to remain undergrazed until livestock levels recover. The variability in rainfall limits the numbers of animals. Pastoralist economies are adapted to exploit this variability. Herders diversify their stock-holdings, with a combination of small stock and camels, or small stock and cattle, to reduce risks, for each species has different requirements. Camels browse taller trees and shrubs; goats browse lower ones; and cattle and sheep graze on grasses. Camels prefer, and benefit from, a more brackish water than cattle and small stock.

Access to grazing land is not a free-for-all in pastoral communities. It is usually managed by agreement among elders. But traditional range-management strategies fall apart if access to land and resources is restricted. It is this that can result in degradation.

## Traditional herding strategies

In general, a livestock-owner will try to maintain a large herd as an insurance against drought years, when animals will die or have to be sold to buy maize. A large herd can be split, with some stock loaned to relatives, to reduce the risk of wholesale loss to disease or drought.

Grazing patterns depend on the season and its rainfall, the immediate needs of the animals, the stock movements of other herders, the presence of ticks and biting flies, security from raiding, and the proximity of water. These changing factors must be constantly re-assessed. When conditions are good, the herder strives for rapid weight-gain and high milk-yields.

During the early dry season, small stock and camels look for remaining green forage and need little or no water. Cattle graze drier pastures. As the dry season progresses, access to water sources becomes more critical, and animals may move much farther from their home range. Camels range farthest afield, within a grazing radius of about 18km from camp; cattle usually stay within 12km, and goats within 8km. Cattle need water every one or two days in a normal dry season, goats and sheep every three days, and camels every seven.

The strategy during a widespread drought is to move stock long distances, often into areas with grazing but far from water sources. For camels this may be 50km, for cattle 30km, and for goats 20km. Stock losses will rise as weaker animals succumb to the two-day journey to water.

Traditionally a destitute family would follow and camp alongside families with herds. After milking, the families with stock would have a whip-round to collect milk for the family without stock. The impoverished herders would take animals on loan when they could, and their neighbours would encourage them to get back on to the ranges with their own herd.

Pastoralist land-use strategies have developed over thousands of years as a means of survival in hostile, unpredictable environments. Foreign donors, national governments, and aid agencies have usually failed to understand the dynamics of indigenous rangeland-management and have tried to alter rather than support traditional practice. The experience of the pastoralists themselves was often ignored.

## On the margins of survival: the Maasai

The Maasai are probably the best-known of Kenya's pastoralists. For centuries they dominated the Central Rift Valley of present-day Kenya and Tanzania, inspiring fear in their neighbours and fascination and respect in early European travellers. Their courage and proud bearing became legendary. Cattle were their life-blood, and agriculture was disdained.

The critical period for the survival of cattle is the rainless months of July to October, when traditionally the Maasai fall back on *dokoya enkishu*, dry-season reserves left ungrazed during the last rains. These reserves are usually upland areas with reliable vegetation. The Maasai do not hunt for food, except in periods of desperate shortage; though in the past the *moran*, or warriors, might hunt a lion or a buffalo, animals which would turn to face the enemy rather than run away.

To colonial administrators and the independent State that succeeded them in Kenya, the Maasai and other pastoralist peoples were deemed an obstacle to progress. A family on the move cannot be easily taxed, educated, or brought into the market economy. For the country's first colonial governor, Sir Charles Eliot, 'the only hope for the Maasai is that under intelligent guidance they may gradually settle down and adopt a certain measure of civilisation'.

The British showed little concern for Maasai rights. Much of the unfenced land that they grazed was taken for white-settler ranching through 'treaties' between the authorities and the chiefs whom they installed. By 1914 the Kenyan Maasai were confined to less than 20 per cent of their former lands, reserves corresponding to today's Narok, Kajiado, and Samburu Districts.

## Pastoralism with a frontier

Amazingly, the Maasai way of life withstood these pressures. But in the last half-century even the remaining Maasai uplands have been taken over for agriculture and wildlife tourism, confining the herders to the poorer margins of their land. Dry-season reserves, perennial water-points, and salt-licks have been lost, with devastating consequences.

With grants from the World Bank, the Kenyan authorities have encouraged privatisation of the remaining Maasai land. As a result, wheat farms, ranches, and irrigated flower farms are displacing the Maasai homesteads and their zebu cattle, leaving the former herders to scrape a living as watchmen and labourers in Nairobi.

The Maasai who remain have no choice but to adapt. Some are beginning to cultivate any remaining lands which will support crops, to safeguard their rights of ownership. At Kimana, in Kajiado District, community leaders have established their own wildlife park with support from the tour company Kuoni; but even if the Maasai do stay on their diminished lands, life must change. Cattle can be only part of a more diverse and more sedentary economy.

## Pastoralist life in the north

The arid northern areas of Kenya, home to the Turkana, Rendille, Somali, Booran, and Gabra people, are less attractive than the Rift Valley region to commercial farmers and the tourism business, because the rains are so poor. Here the main enemy of pastoralists is drought.

Nuria Hujaale is a Somali woman living in Wajir District who lost all her animals in the drought of 1984. She was given 30 goats to help her back on her feet. She recalls, 'As soon as the goats arrived from Oxfam, it began to rain. It was like a blessing. Twenty-six produced young within the year, and by 1991 we had over 250. We were able to help other families with milk loans. We sold male and older female goats to buy clothes and food. We were doing quite well, so we began to exchange some for

cows and camels: eight goats for a cow and twelve for a good young burden camel. We would not have survived the drought of 1992 if we had not been able to sell goats to buy food.'

Nuria's family shares a homestead with five others. It is surrounded by a protective fence of cut thorn. Each family occupies one or two *herios*, domed homes made from arched branches, neatly covered with mats of grass or palm. The door of each *herio* faces towards the thorn enclosure which provides overnight housing for that family's goats. Close by are wigwams of sticks which safely pen the new-born kids.

**left** In nomadic households it is the job of the women to make up the family's *herio* (home) each time a new homestead is established

**left** Tarbaj, Wajir District: Nuria and her son allow the kids to take milk before securing their livestock for the night

Cockerels act as bush alarm clocks to call the family to prayer at dawn. After prayer, the day's work begins with milking. Nuria opens the kid pen and goat enclosure, and one by one calls the lactating goats out to their kids. Each goat responds to her name — Ouley, Bariar, Hale, Harire, Gitama, Bagir, Jogbela — emerging from the flock to supply milk to her kid and to Nuria. After drinking a cup of the warm milk, the boys take the goats out to browse, while the girls help their mother to pound grain for the main meal, which is eaten in the evening after the goats have returned to be milked again.

The basis of pastoralist life in this region is communal land-tenure and communal living. Individual family units depend upon each other for their survival. Lending milk animals within the homestead and to the extended family beyond it produces bonds of mutual obligation which insure families against disaster. These traditional relationships are reinforced by the Islamic moral code, which encourages the redistribution of wealth.

## Kenny Matampash

**Kenny Matampash lives with his family at Oldepe, near Kajiado town. Working with a local voluntary agency, he has encouraged the introduction of hybrid cattle which yield three times the milk of the Maasai zebu. But finding land to graze the cows is becoming increasingly difficult. 'Much of the land is under claim from non-Maasai outsiders: civil servants, army officers, and businessmen. They'll never come to live in this place, but if they can snatch enough, they'll use it to raise bank loans.' Kenny has campaigned to defend Maasai land rights, including the rights of single women, since 1989.**

# Land and poverty

## A communal resource ...

In Kenya, customary patterns of land use and ownership have evolved over time, and they continue to change as Western influences penetrate ever more deeply.

Until colonial times, people did not own land; they had the right to use it, based on their membership of a community. Leaders of communities granted access to land to individuals or families, in return for obligations owed to the group, such as engaging in communal work during the busy harvesting season. An individual's land rights were determined by factors such as sex and age.

In practice, a number of different people had different (and sometimes overlapping) rights to any parcel of land, but none of them had the right to alienate it to anyone else. It was the same in forested areas and pastoralist rangelands: the emphasis was on multiple use by communities, rather than on exclusive ownership by individuals. Land was thus not a commodity in the Western sense. It was held in trust by the living for the benefit of future generations. In the often-quoted words of a Nigerian leader: *Land belongs to a vast family, of which many are dead, few are living, and countless members are still unborn.*

**below** Ole Mbatiany, a Maasai man in Narok District, surveys fenced-off wheat fields where he used to graze his cows

Besides its importance for cultivating crops or supporting livestock, land had many other roles: as spiritual space or political territory, and as a source of building materials, energy, medicines, and water.

It was little wonder, then, that when the British introduced a land-tenure system based on individual titles under English property law, a great deal of conflict and confusion ensued. Kenya has witnessed more experimentation in land reform than any other country in Africa. It began with the Swynnerton Plan of the 1950s and has continued ever since, with a hugely ambitious and costly programme of land titling and registration, much praised by the World Bank. Despite the many problems which this policy has encountered in the agricultural areas of Kenya, it is now being implemented in the pastoral areas, where the consequences have already proved disastrous for the Maasai.

## ... or a privately owned commodity?

The colonial administration regarded the customary land-ownership system as wasteful and inefficient. It set about consolidating scattered holdings and preventing the further subdivision of land. The imagined model of the Swynnerton Plan was the property-owning yeoman farmer of England, employing waged labour. The Plan was quite explicitly designed to create a landed class and a landless class. And that is exactly what it achieved. The necessary programme of social engineering could have taken place only in the context of the suppression of Mau Mau, as the Kikuyu were herded into controlled settlements and so-called 'protected villages', which in reality were more like detention camps. By and large, those who became the landed class were those who had remained loyal to the British, while the Mau Mau fighters were rendered landless.

## 'Telephone farmers' gain ...

A mix of Kenyan smallholders and absentee landowners — dubbed 'telephone farmers' — soon took over most of the former settler farms in the Highlands, with financial help from Britain and the World Bank. Kenya's official policy for land ownership has been *Individualisation, Registration, and Title* (known as 'IRT'). By providing legal freehold title (based on English law) to individuals, and enshrining such transactions in a register, it was — and is — believed that the 'magic of the market' would come into play, and all the imagined evils and inefficiencies of customary communal tenure would be abolished at a stroke. The reality proved to be very different.

## ... but poor smallholders lose out

The people who gained land were almost always male heads of households, because it was only they who were recognised in law. People who had previously enjoyed secondary or subordinate rights to land, especially women and children, rapidly lost out and became increasingly vulnerable. The administration of the system proved to be extremely bureaucratic. It was opaque and open to corruption. It was stacked heavily against those who lacked formal education, and especially the poor.

Acquiring title did not automatically make people eligible for credit, as policy makers had fondly hoped. Most smallholders cannot in fact get credit to help them invest in their land. The local registers have not been maintained efficiently, so they fail to reflect the legal reality. As a result, disputes over land show no signs of abating; in fact, they have increased in areas of severe land-shortage like Central Province.

Equally important is the fact that, despite the attempted introduction of English property law, customary norms, values, and practices have shown remarkable resilience, so the social reality is a complex mix of the two, which is subject to continual tensions. Tenure conversions led to conflict precisely because officials underestimated the strength of community and family controls and the reasons for them: that they guaranteed security of access to land and equity in its distribution, and they ensured that land would be passed down through the generations. In densely populated parts of Kenya, subsequent generations challenged registered titles when attempts were made to extinguish their inheritance rights. With attempts to privatise every piece of land, community grazing grounds disappeared, as did communal sources of wood.

Those who gained most from this process were members of the rural elite and urban businesspeople, who acquired land for speculation or prestige. Those who lost most were the poor and women. Most people would now concede that the results of the programme did not justify the effort and huge resources invested in it.

## Landlessness creates slums

One consequence of land reform, made worse by rapid population growth, was increasing landlessness. Poor farmers who faced some temporary crisis were liable to sell out to the better-off. The result was a massive movement to the towns and cities, especially to Nairobi, where the migrants established 'squatter' slums — despite opposition from the authorities, who occasionally sent in bulldozers to demolish them.

Today it is estimated that 60 per cent of Nairobi's residents are slum dwellers, living in over 100 slums with few services. People living there are highly vulnerable and insecure. Most are self-employed, living on the fringes of society and supporting themselves and their families by engaging in all kinds of activity which are 'off the books' and ignored or condemned by the authorities. Organisations representing the interests of slum dwellers argue the need to legalise their tenure and to recognise their right to basic services such as safe water, proper sanitation, and waste-disposal services.

Urban centres will continue to grow as the landless and stockless poor are forced to migrate to the cities to survive as casual labourers, night-watchmen, petty traders, rag-pickers, beggars, sex workers, and thieves, their sense of dispossession reinforced by the affluent city lifestyles that they see every day but can never attain.

**below** Line Saba, one of the 'villages' of Kibera, Nairobi

# Land and conflict

Since 1991, conflict over the ownership of land has brought displacement and destitution to some 250,000 Kenyan small-holders, who have been attacked and driven off their farms. At least 1,000 people have been killed. The ethnic fault lines which are being exploited by politicians and local power-brokers run along the boundaries of Rift Valley Region in the fertile and densely settled highlands of south-western Kenya. More recently, similar conflicts have broken out on the coast.

It seems that constitutional rights guaranteeing private property and the freedom of citizens to live in any part of Kenya are not worth the paper they are written on. The conflict has severely undermined the legal and political integrity of the tenure system, as people with legal title to land have been chased away from their homes.

In 1996, a report by the Kenya Human Rights Commission condemned government agents for apparently sanctioning the abuses — even in some cases, it was alleged, fanning the violence — and rarely arresting the perpetrators. The clashes began soon after the introduction of multi-party democracy, and those who suffered most were usually members of tribes that were seen to be in opposition to the government. Politicians incited ethnic animosity between so-called indigenous communities, the Kalenjin and Maasai, and those — called migrants or foreigners — who had settled in the area during the colonial era. The Commission concluded that tension still prevailed in almost all the affected areas, and that most victims of the clashes had still not returned to their rightful lands.

The report of the Commission (*Ours By Right, Theirs By Might*, Nairobi 1996) stressed the need for a comprehensive policy to guarantee all citizens' rights to land. It argued that the land problem cannot be effectively solved without thorough and gender-sensitive constitutional reform. It called on the government to meet and listen to representatives of the people, to avoid making inflammatory statements, and to distribute administrative posts more fairly in multi-ethnic areas. It urged the government to stop partitioning provinces and districts on an ethnic basis, which, it said, promotes the myth of tribal exclusiveness.

## Possible reforms

NGOs concerned about the effects of current policies on land in Kenya say there is a need for the following reforms:

- Legal rights for women, allowing them to own property and have access to land; to inherit land as daughters and widows; and to have access to loans, regardless of their marital status.

- A flexible land-tenure regime in which the State acts as a genuine public trustee.

- Policy initiatives aimed at reviving and strengthening traditional practices which supported common property resources.

- Collaboration between State agencies and local institutions in the sustainable management of natural resources.

# Forced evictions: two testimonies

Hundreds of displaced families found refuge in a church compound in Eldoret in 1994. Many were descendants of Kikuyu squatters who had worked on white farms in Rift Valley, and bought plots after Independence. Alice described how her family were driven from their home in Kaptarat farm:

❛ It was on 28 March (1994), just after midnight. The men had stayed awake. They saw fires burning in different directions. Houses were being burnt. We went closer to the Trading Centre to be safe, and the men went to fight. But the warriors were many, and well armed. Some of the men were injured. They had arrow injuries, especially in their hands and legs, and in their bodies. The fighting was still going on, but a lot of the men had joined us, joined the women. They'd dropped out.

The next house to us had just been attacked. They were coming at us from all around. My own house had already been burnt. There were over 200 of us. The police gave us a safe way out. We'd been defeated. We had to leave. They helped us pass from the houses into the Centre. The police gave us protection, but they just watched the houses being burnt.

Before, we shared livestock. We went to each other's ceremonies — weddings, funerals. There wasn't the slightest feeling that we were different tribes. It wasn't multi-partyism that brought this. There was no hostility. It came from outside the community. We'd forgive them, because we have to live with them. But it's difficult to forgive a neighbour who's wearing your clothes and milking your cows. ❜

Priscilla ('I'm so old I can't count how many years it is') sits in the compound at Thessalia Mission in the Rift Valley, surrounded by chairs and kettles salvaged from her bulldozed village, just two kilometres away. She recalls the day in December 1993 when the police arrived to evict her and 600 members of her Luo community from Buru, where the land is now grazed by Kalenjin cattle.

❛ I was cooking. Police came into the house and caned me across the legs. I ran out and made towards the Mission. I fell just near the houses. I saw a tractor bulldozing my house, with everything inside. I lay there a long time until people came to help me, maybe an hour. Staff from the Mission took me to the hospital. My hip was dislocated and I stayed there for three months. Now I'm here. My leg is still not right. ❜

**background and below**
Refugees in their own country:
the camp for displaced people
in Eldoret, 1994

# Health and education — at a price

**right** An informal primary school, Korogocho, Nairobi

Like many African countries, Kenya was determined at Independence to provide better social services for its people than the colonial government had seen fit to offer. Between 1964 and 1979, the number of university students increased 14 times, the number of secondary schools grew almost eight-fold, and the number of primary schools doubled. Over the same period, improvements in health care contributed to a rise in life expectancy from 44 to 55 years.

But these achievements have been threatened in the 1980s and 1990s. Government spending on health services has fallen by one third; programmes of school building and repair have long been abandoned; and structural adjustment reforms have introduced 'user fees' which are taking essential services out of the reach of the poor. Unless the government, with support from donors, can establish a safety net for the poorest, these changes will create an inescapable cycle of poverty for millions of Kenyans.

## A passion for education

The passion for education which grew among Kenyans under colonial rule remains unabated today. Children beg their parents to let them go to school, and no salaried uncle or aunt escapes the call to pay fees for nephews and nieces. With the government's role largely confined to paying teachers' salaries, parental contributions now meet more than one third of the cost of primary and two thirds of the cost of secondary schooling. But the curriculum remains much as it was in colonial times, geared to the education of a privileged elite and producing primary leavers ill-equipped for jobs in agriculture and industry.

Over 80 per cent of primary-age children are enrolled in school, but at secondary level the figure falls below 30 per cent. These

## A school without walls

Throughout Islamic Africa, groups of nomadic
people maintain their own mobile Koranic
schools, which move with the homesteads as
they follow their livestock in search of grazing.
In Kenya, such a school is known as a *dugsi,* and
the religious scholar who teaches the children
to recite the Koran is known as a *maalim.*

A local organisation in Wajir District
is training Koranic teachers to extend their
services by teaching basic literacy and
numeracy to the children and adults of their
homesteads. Teaching aids — a blackboard
and cloth sheets — hang in the trees, and are
designed to be carried easily by camel or
donkey when the community moves on.

In this *dugsi,* Ali Omar Adan, a secondary-
school student, shares the benefit of his
education with his community during the
school holidays. The children learn maths,
music, and reading and writing in English,
Kiswahili, and Kisomali. For two hours each
evening, adults concentrate on literacy and
numeracy, human and animal health, environmental protection, religious instruction, and
civic education. Ali comments: 'They tell me
what they're interested in. It's the women
who ask most of the questions. They have
contributed towards my school fees. I just
want them to have my education. When I
finish, I want to be a teacher.'

## Serah Wanjiru

Serah Wanjiru makes a living as a 'mama mboga', a vegetable woman, hawking produce from door to door in Nairobi's middle-class suburbs. She describes what it means to pay 'user fees' for her four children.

❝ School fees are going up all the time. For Margaret and Garison in primary school I have to pay 1,000Sh each, to cover the costs of non-teaching staff like the watchman and gardener, and to buy materials like chalk. School uniform is another 1,000 each, and books 1,500.

For my first-born boy, Eliud, in Form 4 (secondary), I have to pay 8,800 for the year, and 3,000 in exam fees. For Jane's school I will pay 16,600 for Form 3. That doesn't include uniforms: they can cost 3,000 each for secondary school.

We work hard for our children to get through school, but then there are no jobs, even when they're qualified. Every office you pass, it says "No Work". If you don't know people, you can't get work, even if you're educated. Or you pay bribes. It's the rich who get the jobs. ❞

**right** Dekha, Alasa, and Ethey share one textbook at Khorof Harar Primary School, Wajir District

averages mask huge regional variations: in Kenya's arid regions, primary attendance falls below 30 per cent, and standards of school achievement are usually the lowest in the country. It is often the girls who lose out, leaving school in the later primary years to take on responsibilities in the home. Throughout the country as a whole, fewer than 40 per cent of the girls who start primary school complete the eight-year course. *'Girls are not passing clouds, to be married off at a tender age,'* wrote Diana Omollo, 13 years old, during a class exercise. *'Parents ought to realise that we have a right to education.'*

In Khorof Harar primary school, in the north-eastern district of Wajir, only three of the 28 pupils who recently took the national leaving examination were girls. 'Thousands of families lost their animals in the drought and were forced into Wajir,' commented the head teacher. 'And they are told to build their own schools! Families can't afford books, and the school has no money for them. We just have chalk and talk.' Meanwhile, the children of the rich are driven in limousines to expensive private schools, wearing English-style blazers. Many of the staff are expatriates from the UK. The contrasts between these well-endowed institutions and the wretchedly resourced State schools and Koranic schools vividly demonstrate the divided nature of Kenyan society.

## The health of the nation

Despite cuts in government spending, broad indicators of the nation's health have continued to improve. Life expectancy rose steadily after Independence. Infant mortality has continued to fall to about 70 per thousand births. But the figures disguise huge disparities between urban and rural areas, and between the better-off and the poor. In 1992 almost half of Kenya's rural population was living below the poverty line defined by the World Bank. More than one-third of under-fives in rural areas were stunted in growth due to poor nutrition, compared with one-fifth in urban areas. And by the late 1990s HIV/AIDS was casting a deepening shadow over the lives of many Kenyan families.

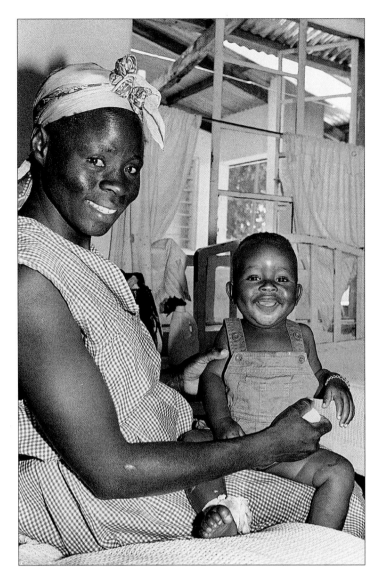

**Desperate measures in a rural health centre**

Efeli Aleri brought her son Joseph to Kima Health Centre, in Vihiga District, weakened by fever and diarrhoea. Seriously dehydrated, he was given an intravenous drip which included quinine to combat his malaria. With further treatment for dysentery, Joseph quickly recovered.

Malaria, anaemia, and diarrhoea are the commonest fatal illnesses among young children in Kenya. Many reach medical help too late to survive, often because their parents

**above** Efeli and Joseph at Kima Health Centre, Vihiga District (Western Province)

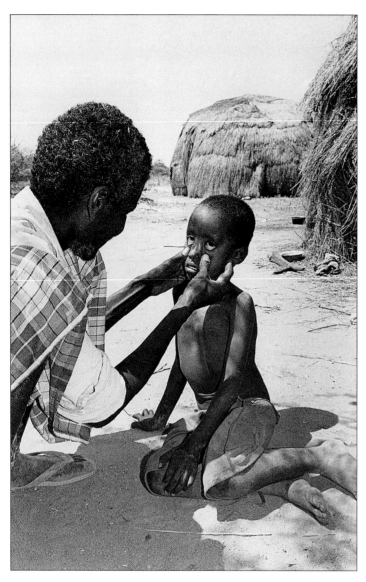

fear bills they can not pay. Though Kima is church-supported, it has had to introduce charges for medicines and treatment, in line with the Ministry of Health's cost-recovery programme. Fees are charged for all in-patient and out-patient services at all hospitals and health centres.

'I took the child to a dispensary near home,' explains Efeli. 'The nurse gave me septrin, just one tablet, and said I should go to Mbale hospital. That's too far for us to travel, so I went to a private pharmacy in our village. I paid 80 shillings [approximately £1.00 at the time] for three injections — I think it was chloroquin. At first Joseph seemed to get better, but then became much worse. I brought him here. I don't know how much I'll have to pay. People who stayed only two days paid 860 shillings. I don't have any money.'

Fred Wekesa, the doctor in charge, explains the dilemmas that this presents. 'The government helps with salaries, but otherwise we have to balance the books. We charge 120 shillings a day for a bed, 550 shillings for a delivery — 750 if it's a first-born — and so on. When a child like Joseph begins to recover, we begin to negotiate. We might ask a patient to leave something, like this radio: we didn't buy it for the hospital, we're just keeping it until the owner pays. If people really can't pay, we will waive fees.'

## Prevention is cheaper than cure

Because of the high cost of curative hospital-based care, centres like Kima, with support from the government and NGOs, have placed increasing emphasis on preventive health care in the community. Kima has for many years organised a mobile outreach clinic for mother and child health-care. In 1985 staff began to train volunteer community health workers, and during the 1990s encouraged local villages to begin to take more responsibility for their own development. Several have formed committees, taking forward ideas to improve food production through organic farming, to protect and improve water sources, and encourage credit and loan schemes.

Rose Omuyoma has worked as a traditional birth attendant since 1978, and now reports to her village development committee in Esisimi,

**above** Riba, Wajir District: Kanyare Wardere, a community health volunteer, examines Mohamed Abdullah, who has been suffering from diarrhoea and malaria

**right** Rose Omuyoma (left) advising Ana Abwacho on the use of contraceptive pills, Esisimi Village, Vihiga District

**left** A barber's shop in Vihiga town: as AIDS awareness has grown, the use of condoms has increased

near Kima. She has no doubt that life has improved. 'When I started, there was a lot of malnutrition. Many children died from whooping cough and measles. Babies would be eating porridge, even ugali, at three months. Our drinking water was dirty. These days, far fewer children die. We have immunisation, clean water and better food, and people are spacing their children.'

Rose finds that more and more of her time is spent giving advice on family planning. 'Nowadays, now that they're informed, women are interested. Before, women even had ten children. Now most feel that six is enough, or even just three or four. It's partly because the cost of living is so high — schooling is expensive, and so is food.'

## The impact of AIDS

The impact of the AIDS epidemic on life in Kenya now dwarfs most other concerns.

By the end of 1996 an estimated 1.25 million Kenyans were infected by HIV, most of them men and women under 30 years of age. Personal tragedy is compounded by the social and economic devastation that hits communities through the loss of large numbers of young adults. Worst affected are Nairobi and Western Kenya, where studies in 1995 revealed that over 25 per cent of pregnant women attending ante-natal clinics were HIV-positive.

Though government response was initially slow, the Minister of Health declared AIDS a national disaster in 1993. At first campaigns focused on raising public awareness about HIV. But people's behaviour is rooted in their society, culture, and economic status, and is not easily changed. The speed with which HIV has spread reflects the breakdown of customary sanctions in a rapidly changing society, and the powerlessness of the poor, the unemployed, and of women. Studies suggest that a combination of fatalism and psychological denial makes the prospect of illness and death in ten years' time unlikely to discourage today's pleasures. Girls and women often have little choice in the matter: rape is commonplace, and their dependent role, inside and outside marriage, can leave them trading sex for short-term survival.

The government, the UN, and a host of Kenyan and international non-government organisations (NGOs) now support prevention and care programmes. In 1994 the Kenyan AIDS NGOs Consortium (KANCO) was formed to help co-ordinate the work and practice of hundreds of small and large NGOs. Some of the most promising initiatives are in youth-to-youth work, in which young people develop the understanding, social skills, and self-esteem they need to control their own sexual health. In effect they are also redefining their ideas about relationships between men and women.

One such scheme has been developed by the Mathare Youth Sports Association (MYSA). MYSA was founded in 1987 to promote social responsibility through sporting activities. Some indication of the size of Nairobi's largest shanty, Mathare Valley, is provided by the fact that by 1997 this association included 410 boys' teams and 170 girls' teams. The girls' teams were not established without a struggle, but they have proved successful in helping to change attitudes about the roles and status of women and girls. The club also tackles AIDS education by training young people, including the best footballers — who are influential role-models in the community — to spread the message to other young people.

Sarah started playing football five years ago, when she was 9 years old. In 1996 she was able to travel to Norway with her team, to take part in the annual Norway Cup. As well as playing football, Sarah takes part in neighbourhood clean-ups, referees matches, coaches younger teams, and talks to players about the threat of AIDS. 'I'm proud of my teams. The boys look on me as a sister, and I treat them like my brothers. They know I've got other interests in life and they respect me for that. In fact, playing football has helped me to get to know boys as friends. It's given me the confidence to say "no" to boys who are interested in sex.'

**below** A rally in Nairobi protesting about violence against women

# City
# in the sky

Nairobi, the capital of Kenya, is the largest city between Cairo and Johannesburg. It dominates the communications, trade, and industry of East Africa. Its shining high-rise monuments to commerce and tourism create a mini-Manhattan, declaring their allegiances along the crowded sky-line: Lonhro, Barclays Plaza, British Airways, Norwich Union, Kenya Airways, Serena Hotel.

Conversations in English, Kiswahili, and Kikuyu are heard at every shaded street corner, interrupted by the horn blasts of traffic jamming the side streets. Fortunately for the motorist, the city's broad main street, Kenyatta Avenue, was laid out to allow a team of 12 oxen to turn about. A few remnants of those early colonial times survive, characterised by the

District Commissioner's Office of 1913, its grey stonework and once-imposing pillared entrance now crowded into insignificance by the twenty-storey backdrop of Nyayo House and the eight-lane highway at its doorstep.

Much of the city-centre's business is tourist-driven: the banks and money exchanges, gem shops and galleries of African art, one-hour photo-processing shops, and hawkers selling their bracelets and carvings. Bookshops display the works that have helped to glamorise Kenya: *Out of Africa*, *The Flame Trees of Thika* and its sequels, the books of Hemingway and the Adamsons and the lifelong traveller Wilfred Thesiger.

The Hilton is one of a cluster of luxury hotels, including the venerable Norfolk and the New Stanley with its pavement café, The Thorn Tree,

**above** Kenyatta Avenue, Nairobi

where tourists take refuge from Africa at prices which only they will pay, write their postcards, and consult their travel books. The acacia tree around which the café is built carries a four-sided board covered in notes left by modern Livingstones and Stanleys who enjoy a less hazardous passage through Africa.

*Peugeot 505 drivers,*
*hope you made it from Blantyre.*

*Looking for lift north — Ethiopia, Eritrea,*
*Djibouti, Egypt.*

*Dorothy, come home soon — Mum.*

*Finlay MacMillan, proceed as planned,*
*but avoid Chancellor Kohl look-alikes.*

Beyond this modern facade is a city of intimidating contrasts. Before Independence, residential development was racially segregated, as in most colonial cities. To the west lie the leafy suburbs of Langata and Karen, where Europeans recreated their homeland under a perennial sun; to the north lie the airy hillside estates of Runda, Loresho, Muthaiga, and Spring Valley; to the east a mixture of orderly new estates and sprawling concrete blocks, creeping out towards the international airport.

Squeezed between these expanding suburbs and the city centre are the overcrowded shanties. No one knows how many people live in these unplanned settlements: the largest, Mathare Valley and Kibera, may each be home to more than half a million. Estimates of the city's population range wildly from 2.4 to 4.2 million.

## Cardboard city

On the streets of Nairobi, boys as young as six, matchstick-thin, meander and stagger around, their eyes half-closed, clutching balls of rag soaked in paint-thinner. Like the coca chewed in Peru, or the *miraa* in Somalia, it dulls the pangs of hunger.

Adults are more likely to turn to *changaa*, the illicit low-cost local spirit. Rape is not unusual in the tightly packed settlements, and prostitution is one of the necessary means of scraping a living. AIDS and other sexually transmitted diseases are rampant. Crime is such a problem in the shanties that those who are caught or suspected risk being burned to death by mobs.

Individual sponsorship, to school or vocational training, opens the door for some to escape. But new arrivals pour in relentlessly from the rural areas and from Nairobi's low-income estates, where rents are rising all the time.

## Street children

Some of the children who eke out a living on the streets of the city have a home of sorts to return to at night. Others live in *chuoms*, small communities sleeping in cardboard boxes in alleyways.

A development worker in Nairobi describes their situation: 'There are hideouts in town where they sleep, perhaps 30 boys and girls together. They play families: each little girl has a "husband". At night, when the boys are getting ready to sleep, the girls are getting ready to work. Even the people who live and work in Nairobi don't realise there are so many girls there, because they are only visible at night. Men are going for these young ones, the 9–13 year olds, because they feel it's safer. But many of the girls have sexually transmitted diseases and are HIV-positive. Some of these children are so intelligent and determined to get on in life. When we ask them what they most want, *education* is first on every child's list. Second is *love*: they want someone who will care for them.

'Usually the problem that brings children on to the streets is with the families and the communities, so we have to work with them. Some communities have just given up. Others have real cohesion, even though they are slums, and the children don't leave. They have to belong to the community, not just the family.'

Many organisations are working to improve living conditions in Nairobi's slums, from small local self-help and church groups to the Kenyan authorities, international NGOs, and donor governments.

# St Luke's ROCK group

St Luke's is a small church close to Kenyatta market on the fringe of Kibera. Every day about 50 children come to school here, to a class run by volunteers in the shade of an acacia. On Saturdays and Sundays, when school is out, the children still come early in the morning to play in the dusty church grounds. For the boys rolling tyres along the paths, the girls skipping and hop-scotching in the shade, and those who, unexpectedly, lie in quiet discussion on the grass, it is the emptiness and quiet that bring them to the compound. In Kibera the landlords leave only enough space between the houses for a person to pass.

Every Saturday the women of ROCK — Rescue Our Children Kenyatta — also come together under the acacia to make their plans. The Chairwoman, Jane Wanjiru, explains the group's business plans. 'We began by contributing 10 shillings each week [about 15 pence at the time], then 20 and now 100. So far we have saved 32,000. Our project is a water point. We'll buy the tank and pipes and pay for them to be fitted, and for the City Council to install a meter. Once we have an income from selling water, we may move on to installing a kerosene pump.'

The residents of Kibera have to buy their water from privately installed pipelines, at a price set by market forces. The base price is 2Sh for 20 litres, but this rises during times of shortage to 10Sh, several times more than a middle-class householder would pay for mains supply.

Two-thirds of the women in ROCK are single parents. Many scrape a living in the middle-class neighbourhoods which surround Kibera, cooking, washing, and nannying for approximately £1.00 a day, or hawking vegetables from door to door. In Kibera itself there is petty trade in foodstuffs, daily commodities like soap, charcoal, and kerosene, and in illicit brews like *changaa.*

Women are the backbone of life in the shanties. Many arrive as single parents, disinherited by separation from their husbands. For others, the rigours of living in poverty erode relationships and lay bare the foundations of the family, breaking the spirit of most men and revealing in many of the women a remarkable tenacity to hold together a home for their children.

**left** Njeri Wanjohi, a member of ROCK, has lived in Kibera since 1971, raising her 8 children in this single room

**below** Christmas party organised by the local Asian community for children at St Luke's Church, Nairobi

# Tales of city life

**right** Mwangi and his sister Wangui trying to earn a few shillings in Uhuru Park, Nairobi, in 1994

**below** Wangui outside her boarding primary school, Limuru, in 1998

## Mwangi's story

Mwangi lives in Line Saba, one of the nine 'villages' that make up the shanty town of Kibera, in Nairobi. He is known locally as 'Parking Mwangi', because he used to earn a few shillings by helping drivers to park at the busy Kenyatta market. His mother, who brought her five children to Nairobi when she lost her home and land in Central Province, recently died of an AIDS-related illness; the children have lost contact with their father. At the age of 16,

Mwangi became responsible for the future of his four younger sisters.

One of them, Wangui, has been lucky: she has been sponsored to attend a boarding primary school in Limuru, where she is regularly placed in the top five of her year. The eldest girl, Wanjiru, looks after Muthoni and Beria while Mwangi scrapes a living for them all by washing cars and clearing garbage. Occasionally, to make ends meet, Mwangi will spend 120 shillings on a litre of paint-thinner — the drug of choice among street-children. *Poverty knows no morals* is a catchphrase often heard in Kenya. *Poverty has no choice* might be more apt. With care, Mwangi can retail the can, shilling by shilling, for 300 shillings. His aim is to take Muthoni and Beria back to their father's village, so that they can start school. 'It just needs 1,800 shillings to get them started. School is cheaper in the rural areas. Then I have to get money to build a house there.' For himself, Mwangi dreams of training to become a mechanic or a driver; if the chance ever comes, he will seize it.

## The street photographer

Bernard is at his 'office', marked only by the concrete block that serves as a seat, at 8.30 every morning. Seven days a week, 365 days a year. He leaves when the equatorial sun sets at 6 pm. Bernard makes his living as a 'street photographer' in Uhuru Park, working a pitch by the main road not far from the Nyayo monument commemorating Kenya's independence, near to the roundabout where the traffic on Kenyatta Avenue and Uhuru Highway meets — and often collides. Bernard is frequently called on to take photos for insurance claims.

Customers are regular, often coming every month or two for portraits against the different backdrops offered by the park, its monument, and the fringe of high-rise buildings. Bernard is even an employer, taking on an assistant to tout for business and look after customers while he is busy taking pictures around the park, or hurrying to the processing lab. He pays his apprentice, Mwamba, 100Sh a day.

Ten years on one of the busiest pathways in Africa have made Bernard a natural communicator. His face moves expressively as he speaks, his frequent overstatement acknowledged by a broad, lingering smile. He is also the Park's Number One philosopher, an avid reader of any magazines he can lay his hands on. He can give you fine detail on the history of the Palestine–Iraeli rapprochement, or Uganda's relationship with Rwanda since 1986, or the Lancaster House negotiations which secured independence for Kenya. 'Things were different then. Uhuru Highway was Government Road, and no Africans were allowed to pass.'

## The taxi-driver

Business with officialdom in Kenya usually requires 'a small something', or *chai* (tea), as it used to be termed. This explains why cars, buses, and even aeroplanes can keep running until they fall apart.

The oldest and roughest-looking vehicles in Nairobi are the taxis. Looking too worn-out even for the wreckers' yard, they cough and rattle their way around the capital, a testimony to the 'small something' that can procure a permit or a licence for anything or anyone.

above
Bernard in his 'office'

Most cabs lack lights and seatbelts; windscreens are splintered and tyres worn down.

Richard has been driving taxis for two years, working in 36-hour shifts. He works every day and every other night. He has a proper licence now, though for years he drove with a fake, which cost him 5,000Sh on the black market — cheaper than taking the test. Recently, hoping to find work as a long-distance lorry-driver, Richard applied for a passport. 'On the form it said 400 shillings,' he complains, 'but I had to go from office to office, and those offices ate almost 9,000.'

## The shoesmith and his wife

Edmund, Marceline, and their three children, aged 2 to 6, live in a single room in Dandora, a suburb of Nairobi. It is in a terrace of iron-roofed sheds facing on to a small walled compound. The room is divided by two hanging sheets, screening the two beds. The family cannot afford electricity, which would add a couple of hundred shillings to the monthly rent, paid through an agent to an absentee landlord.

Here, on the concrete floor, Edmund can make up small orders for shoes. For larger orders he pays rent to share the workshop of another shoesmith. He does work on contract and gets paid 60Sh for each pair completed. He can produce five pairs of shoes on a good day. The contractor sells each pair for about KSh500 to shops in town, where they are resold for KSh700–800. Edmund has tendered successfully for large orders of shoes; but, without capital or credit, he cannot buy enough material to fulfil the requirements.

His wife Marceline works in catering at City Hall, cooking for civil servants. She receives the national minimum wage, equivalent in 1996 to £35.00 per month. After deduction for hospital insurance and National Security, she takes home 2,600Sh. Paying a rent of 1,500Sh per month, and a monthly bus fare of 600Sh, Marceline has only 500Sh left from her salary. This, together with Edmund's irregular earnings, has to meet all of the family's other needs.

## The double disadvantage

Kenya's second city and premier port, Mombasa, has the atmosphere of a street bazaar, a cosmopolitan mix of Africa and Arabia. Lacking the investment that has transformed central Nairobi, the town's flaking blend of Arab and colonial architecture was designed on a human scale. The life of the town spills out over the pavements and roads, the shaded shopfronts obscured by the stalls of vendors. People throng the streets late into the evening, shopping or just talking, long after the workers of Nairobi have fled the threatening streets for the safety of their homes.

In Mombasa there is a fine tradition of institutional provision for disabled people. But institutions can constrain as well as liberate the spirit; negative attitudes towards disability leave disabled people doubly disadvantaged in a country where opportunities for education, health care, and jobs are already very limited.

### Jennifer's story

Jennifer earns a living — of sorts — by sewing stuffed elephants for the tourist trade. She is paid 45Sh for each elephant — which is sold for 310Sh in the shops. Though she walks easily enough with a leg brace, others' perceptions of her disability are enough to limit her job opportunities to a sheltered workshop.

'I was born in 1969 in Murang'a. When I was eight months old I had polio. I went to primary school and did two years at high school, but I couldn't afford to continue, as we are six children.

'I did the tailoring course at Mathare Youth Polytechnic. When I left, I was afraid to look for a job. People advertise that they need a tailor; you go, and they just look at you head to toe and say they already have someone. They only look at my disability.

'When I go for interviews, they ask me different questions, the wrong questions. I want to be asked the same questions as everyone else, so that I can pass or fail like anyone else. But they ask me, "How will you be coming to work? Can you walk around? Who'll be helping you? Who'll take you?" It's so discouraging. We have no rights. If you go to a supermarket, or even for an office appointment, the guard will stop you entering. He says, "There's no begging here." If you are disabled, they think you must be a beggar.

'I'm a member of the Kenya Society of Physically Handicapped (KSPH). There are benefits — not with money, but in getting to know about your rights, and how to fight and keep pride. So it's good to be inside. KSPH gives me a voice.'

## Patrick's story

Like Jennifer, Patrick Makallo contracted polio as a child. After completing school, he trained in accountancy, and now runs a successful leather-working business, employing 20 women home-workers in the production of tourist souvenirs. 'Beadwork is not my profession,' he smiles, 'but I have to make a living. No one will create a vacancy for you if you are disabled. I can't wait the time it might take for me to become an accountant.'

Patrick recalls the frustrations of his boyhood: 'Boys of 12 and 13 would go out to hunt. They'd just decide, "Let's go", and collect each other and go off. I would want to go with them, but of course I couldn't. They might be away for a week, and when they came back: "Look, look what we've killed!" They could even kill buffalo and elephant. Now that's been stopped, but then you weren't a man if you didn't go to hunt. But I was gifted with a catapult! I was a sharpshooter. I could knock mangoes out of the tree, even coconuts. The birds feared me.

'But when I went to Kenyatta Secondary School, I found that other boys could understand me, we could make friendship. I had close friends and we shared all our ideas. My best friend was Lawrence. We're still in touch. But the other boys would sneak out to meet girls, and I couldn't. The girls wouldn't look at me. If they did come over to talk, their friends would tease them. You're not free when you're disabled. Now we have wives who understand us ... serious relationships are

different! But disabled girls don't get married so easily. Women have so many jobs to do in the home. No man is prepared to marry if he is the one who has to fetch water.'

Patrick too is active in KSPH, and was recently elected to the post of Secretary General of the Coast branch.

**above** Jennifer acting as an interpreter between deaf and hearing friends, Mombasa

**left** Patrick making a belt at his 'workshop' on a Mombasa street corner

# Culture old and new

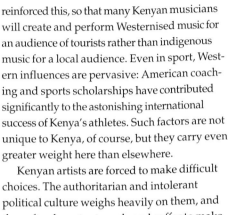

**W**estern influences pervade Kenyan culture. For the ruling elite, being Western is equated with being modern. So a theatregoer in Nairobi is far more likely to encounter a play by a British or North American author than an African work. Similarly, bookshops are full of books romanticising the colonial past and the role of the settlers. The impact of tourism has reinforced this, so that many Kenyan musicians will create and perform Westernised music for an audience of tourists rather than indigenous music for a local audience. Even in sport, Western influences are pervasive: American coaching and sports scholarships have contributed significantly to the astonishing international success of Kenya's athletes. Such factors are not unique to Kenya, of course, but they carry even greater weight here than elsewhere.

Kenyan artists are forced to make difficult choices. The authoritarian and intolerant political culture weighs heavily on them, and they often have to struggle and suffer to make their voices heard. Kenya's best-known writer, Ngugi wa Thiong'o, was imprisoned for his views and wrote graphically about his experiences in *Detained — A Writer's Prison Diary*. Ngugi's early writings are a far more accurate portrayal of colonial life than those of Elspeth Huxley or Robert Ruark. He confronted the dilemma facing every African author — 'For whom do I write?' — by deciding in 1977 to abandon writing in English and write instead in his native Gikuyu. From this point, when he began to reach a wider and more popular grassroots audience, the authorities clamped down on him more vigorously. Ironically, Ngugi's international repute is such that his works are immediately translated into English. Dominant themes in much Kenyan literature, whatever the language, are the clashes between local and foreign cultures and between the past and the present.

## Local and oral culture

In Kenya there is a vibrant tradition of community theatre, in which locally written plays, often implicitly critical of the values and lifestyles of the elite, are performed before large and enthusiastic audiences. The Travelling Theatre of the University of Nairobi played an important role in strengthening this tradition.

**below** Samburu District: playing *bao*, a game popular throughout Kenya

Indeed, the culture of oral tradition generally is sufficiently strong that in the 1980s writers like Ngugi, Okot p'Bitek, and Taban lo Liyong were able to get oral culture included in the syllabuses of schools, colleges, and universities, in the face of much opposition.

Oral traditions, which include folk tales, legends, myths, songs, poems, tongue-twisters, puns, jokes, proverbs, riddles, and rituals, are alive and well, not just some relic from the past. Children learn manners, customs, and history through stories and songs recited in the evenings, usually at the home of a grandmother or other older woman. Adults and children come together, and all can join in the telling.

In 1988, traditional music was introduced into schools and colleges, on the recommendation of a Presidential National Music Commission, which took evidence from more than 10,000 people. Kenya has a rich history in traditional music, both as a recreation and, especially in the 1930s and 1950s, in the form of revolutionary political songs. Today there is an annual music festival for schools and churches which brings together many different forms of music. Ngoma (drum and dance) music is the oldest tradition. It uses local languages and dance rhythms and is played at weddings, births, and funerals. There is also a distinctive Swahili musical tradition.

In terms of modern popular music, because instruments are so expensive, Kenyan musicians are generally out of work, though Nairobi's recording studios attract musicians from far afield. Reggae music is very popular, and its derivatives hip-hop, slow-jam, funk, and lingala.

## Sport

Sport in Kenya mirrors the divisions of class and ethnicity. Football is the people's sport, and teams have traditionally had ethnic identities. Though the explicit labels have been banned, the associations remain. Cricket is for the elite — which did not prevent a sense of great pride when Kenya beat the West Indies in the 1996 World Cup.

Athletes such as Kip Keino and Henry Rono and current stars such as Moses Kiptanui, Wilson Kipketer, and Daniel Komen have earned Kenya a wealth of Olympic medals in middle- and long-distance events. Joyce

**below** Runners competing in the Nairobi half-marathon

### Maasai proverbs

*One finger will not kill a louse.*

*The stick on the hearth laughs at the stick in the fire.*

*One cattle-gate is not large enough for two elders.*

*There is no gecko that does not claim to have the longest tail.*

Chepchumba won the Women's London Marathon in 1997. Running (like boxing for black Americans) offers a route out of poverty for those lucky enough to attract the attention of coaches. This is even more the case now that overt professionalism has replaced 'shamateurism', and some Kenyans are able to demand high appearance fees for agreeing to run in major events overseas. Some have even opted to live and train abroad.

# The impact of tourism

Kenya is widely renowned for its wildlife parks and the coral-fringed beaches of its Indian Ocean coastline. Tourism has become big business for Kenya in the age of the jumbo jet, the package tour, and shrinking holiday horizons. After agriculture, it is the largest source of foreign exchange. Tourism accounts for 19 per cent of Gross Domestic Product and employs several hundred thousand people. In 1996 there were about 720,000 foreign visitors — some way short of the government's target of 1.2m for the mid-1990s. Around 100,000 travel from the United Kingdom each year.

The industry faces increasing competition from 'the new South Africa' and Tanzania (whose beaches and game parks are less crowded), and is affected by concerns about AIDS and crime.

The leisure industry was in crisis in late 1997, after politically motivated violence in the coastal towns killed more than 60 people — none of them tourists — and forced an estimated 100,000 to flee from their homes. The impact on tourism was devastating: charter flights and hotel bookings were cancelled, and thousands of workers laid off.

## Chief Nkonina Songoi

❛ Tourists pass through here constantly, from one Park to another. We have no relationship with them. They come and leave, knowing nothing of us. If someone is dying by the road, they don't stop. They knock down calves and goats and don't stop. These people must be human. It's our land they cross to get to the Park. Surely they must stop and talk to us if they kill an animal.

Wildlife coming out of the Parks — particularly Amboseli — are all over our land now. They don't ask permission. But if we cross into the Park with our cattle, the Rangers chase us out with Land Rovers and helicopters. These hills are our dry-season grazing. We have to take our herds there, or they will die. But the tourists complain to the Rangers that they see too many cows in the Park. Then the helicopter comes. ❜

## Giving the tourists what they want

The government is trying to diversify the leisure industry, steering tourists away from 'beach and safari' packages by developing golf courses, lake cruises, and health spas based on geo-thermal springs. But Maasai Mara, at the northern tip of the great Serengeti plains, is still a huge attraction, host to the dramatic annual migration of more than one million wildebeest. The vast herds arrive on this favoured grassland at the height of the dry season and return south with the onset of the rains, pouring across the Mara River — a spectacle that tourists can, for a price, watch from the silent vantage of a hot-air balloon. The presence of wildebeest in the food chain ensures high numbers of lions and leopards, as well as hyenas and other scavengers.

In all there are now over 50 game parks and reserves, occupying almost 8 per cent of Kenya's land surface, dedicated to conservation and profit. The first parks were created in the late 1940s, to conserve the wildlife depleted by white hunters, though game shoots continued until 1977. The figure of the Maasai *moran*, or warrior, resting with his weight on one leg, spear in hand, is used as a symbol of the parks and lodges. In contrived homesteads, called 'cultural bomas', tourists are entertained by Maasai dancers and buy carvings and batiks depicting Maasai life.

But the Maasai and their northerly cousins, the Samburu, were thrown off these grasslands when the parks were established. With their cattle they had lived for centuries alongside the teeming wildlife of the plains, following the rains and the grazing like the wildebeest. Ironically it is in the name of conservation that they have been excluded from their traditional water-holes, salt-licks, and dry-season grazing.

Other reserves are well known from books and TV documentaries: Amboseli at the foot of Africa's highest mountain, snow-capped Kilimanjaro; Lake Nakuru with its pink mist of flamingoes; and Meru, 'Elsa country', made famous by Joy Adamson and her lions. But the biggest attraction remains the Maasai Mara.

## KWS: managing people and conservation

Wildlife is one of Kenya's most important natural assets, and wildlife tourism is worth US$350 million a year, nearly half the value of the total Kenyan tourist industry. Yet, during the 1980s, poaching threatened to destroy one of its major attractions. The profits to be made

**below** The privatisation of land threatens to prevent wildlife from moving freely across the Rift Valley grasslands

from illegal wildlife products, especially ivory and rhino horn, reduced the numbers of elephants from 160,000 to 20,000, and rhinos were virtually wiped out: there are now fewer than 1,000 remaining in Kenya.

The urgent need for conservation prompted the creation of the Kenya Wildlife Service (or KWS, as it is generally known) in the late 1980s. KWS is responsible for managing Kenya's wildlife resources, separately from the Ministry of Tourism and Wildlife. Under the leadership of Richard Leakey, KWS adopted tough measures to stamp out poaching and was largely successful in curbing the mass destruction of wildlife.

KWS, employing some 3,500 staff, now faces new challenges in identifying and maintaining a viable economic role for wildlife. Wildlife management remains a key form of land use in areas of marginal agricultural value. Wildlife tourism offers great economic potential, but most of the benefits go to foreign and private Kenyan owners and tourist operators, to the government, and to people employed directly in the industry. Very little benefit from one of the most valuable sectors of the Kenyan economy goes to poor people in rural areas, and especially pastoralist communities. Apart from a few projects on communal (or 'group') ranches near Amboseli and in Laikipia, there are still very few examples of tourist facilities owned and operated by the local community. Instead, the people who live closest to wildlife are reduced to selling trinkets and doing 'cultural performances' for tourists, for which they might earn the equivalent of £1 a day.

KWS has developed a policy of revenue-sharing, intended to ensure that those who live closest to the wildlife and who are potentially the most effective conservers of it receive direct benefits. Nevertheless, KWS and some of the non-government organisations concerned with conservation recognise that, without rights to the use of wildlife, people in local communities are not likely to enjoy a share in the revenue or benefits, or to help ensure the conservation of this valuable national asset. Through projects like the 'Partnership Programme', KWS is trying to explore ways to develop wildlife management and community benefits, but this ambitious scheme is still at an early stage, and there are many obstacles in its path.

## Johnson Pesi

‘ Tourism has completely changed our lives. Some of the Maasai were very poor till they came here; now they can buy clothes for themselves, and some have even bought cows. So there have been some advantages for us. But there are disadvantages too. Sometimes tourists take lots of photographs, and some are completely pornographic. Sometimes they photograph someone who is not dressed properly; then they go and display it in their country, which is a big damage to our culture. I don't understand why they should want to do it, and I feel very uncomfortable about being photographed.

There is not much exchange between us. We don't tell the tourists about our culture, and they don't tell us about theirs. We don't sell them what we own: we make something similar to what we own, especially to be sold. The songs we sing for tourists are not the real songs that we sing during our own ceremonies, so they don't affect our culture. It's just a fake thing for tourists.

I am dressed as a *moran* (Maasai warrior). But I'm not yet a *moran;* I'm preparing to become one: I'm growing my hair. There are no real *morans* here. They are away eating meat at the meat-eating camps, so we have to act until they come back; then we'll go away.

The land of the Maasai Mara which was turned into a national reserve must have been sold unknowingly by our people. We are trying to see if we can compensate ourselves by collecting money from tourists. ’

63

# The promise of prosperity

Compared with many other African nations, Kenya has an abundance of natural assets and economic opportunities. Yet for millions of Kenyans the promises which Independence offered remain unfulfilled, and the struggle for social, economic, civil, and political rights is still to be won. Drought, floods, lack of land, high prices for basic necessities, and — since the late 1980s — conflict and violence combine to make life very harsh for poor people.

History will reveal the true significance of the 1997 Presidential elections, which produced a third five-year term for President Moi and the KANU government. The prospects for peace, prosperity, and equality remain uncertain. What will need to change in order to give real hope to the kind of people whose opinions are represented in this book? Their future depends upon the implementation of policies which will achieve prosperity with equity; governance which upholds the law and recognises people's basic rights; stability and the means to ensure food security; access to land and security of tenure; and eco-nomic measures which will prevent the blight of urban destitution for children, youth, and women.

Will the radical upheavals, both violent and peaceful, which have affected nearby countries be reproduced in Kenya itself? The stability of Kenya continues to be a vital ingredient of wider regional prosperity and progress in Africa. If IMF demands for economic reform and the elimination of corruption are upheld, donor governments may yet call for a change of tune from the KANU regime. It remains to be seen whether this call will be accompanied by demands for the eradication of poverty and an end to the abuses of human and civil rights that threaten the well-being of millions of ordinary Kenyans.

Despite their persistent and growing disadvantages, the fortitude of Kenya's desperately poor people means that there are very real opportunities for change. Above all, maintaining peace remains the biggest challenge. For the foreseeable future, there are no simple solutions for Kenyans and those who continue to support them.

**right** Street scene in Loitokitok, Kajiado District

## Thomas Lugalya

❝ Let me not lie to you.

Kenyans are peaceful.

Enough blood was shed for Independence,
and we do not want to shed more.

How can you live with people for ten years,
twenty years, then fight them?

I like my country very much.

If we worked hard and stopped
slipping money into our pockets,
we could be as good as America or Britain.

If we work together.

Unity is important.

We have milk and honey flowing,
but we do not know how to tap them. ❞

*Thomas Lugalya, a 22 year-old musician
with* The Ghetto Ruffians, *Nairobi*

# Kenya: dates and events

**50 BC:** First written record of life on the East African coast.

**8th century AD:** First contact with Muslim traders from Arabian Peninsular and Iran.

**14th and 15th centuries:** Flourishing of Swahili coastal towns on Indian Ocean trade routes.

**1510:** Portuguese sacking of Swahili coastal towns.

**1698:** Mombasa and other coastal towns captured from the Portuguese by Arabs, who remained in control until the 19th century.

**1840–90:** The slave trade at its height in the Kenyan interior.

**1885–86:** The Congress of Berlin divided East Africa between Britain and Germany.

**1895:** Kenya declared a British protectorate

**1896–1901:** Building of the Uganda Railway from Mombasa to Lake Victoria; British conquest of Kenya.

**1903–14:** Settlers began to acquire land in the Highlands; eviction of Maasai and Kikuyu.

**1914–18:** Thousands of Kenyans conscripted into the World War I campaign against the Germans in Tanganyika.

**1920s:** Beginning of political struggles.

**1939–45:** Thousands of Kenyans fought in World War II, as far afield as Burma.

**1944:** Formation of the Kenya African Union (KAU).

**1946:** Jomo Kenyatta returned from England, having left Kenya in 1931; became President of KAU in the following year.

**1952:** State of Emergency declared. Start of the Mau Mau uprising. Kenyatta arrested, tried, imprisoned.

**1953–55:** All political parties banned.

**1954:** Swynnerton Plan to consolidate land holdings.

**1960:** Formation of Kenya African National Union (KANU) and Kenya African Democratic Union (KADU).

**1961:** Kenyatta released from prison and became President of KANU.

**1963:** Independence achieved on 12 December, with Kenyatta as first Prime Minister.

**1964:** Kenya became a Republic, with Kenyatta as first President. KADU dissolved itself.

**1978:** Death of Kenyatta; Daniel arap Moi became second President.

**1982:** Attempted military coup by the air force.

**1987:** Constitutional changes gave greater powers to Moi.

**1989:** Tea overtook coffee as Kenya's main export earner.

**1991:** Ethnic clashes over land broke out in the Rift Valley.

**1992:** First national multi-party elections since Independence. Moi and KANU defeated divided rivals.

**1997:** Second national multi-party elections preceded by widespread violence, in which many people died. Daniel arap Moi won third term of office.

# Kenya: facts and figures

**Area:** 582,646 sq km

**Proportion of arable land:** 8%

**Population:** 32 million (1996 UN estimate)

**Main ethnic groups:** Kikuyu 21%, Luhya 14%, Luo 12%, Kalenjin 11%, Kamba 11%, Kisii 6%, Meru 5%, Mijikenda 5%, Maasai 2%. Plus c. 30 other groups, including Asians, Europeans, and Arabs, totalling 12% — figures from 1989 census (regarded as controversial).

**Official languages:** English and Swahili

**Religions:** Christian 70%, Animist 19%, Muslim 6%, Other 5%

**Population growth rate:** 3.4% per annum

**Urban population:** 26% (1995)

**Adult literacy:** 78% (1995)

**School enrolment:** 92% primary, 29% secondary (1993)

**Average life expectancy:** 55 (female), 52 (male) (1994)

**Child mortality:** 73 per 1,000 live births (1996) (UK: 9 per 1,000)

**Currency:** Kenya Shilling (KSh) = 100 cents; KSh20 = 1 Kenya pound (K£)

**Exchange rate:** KSh56: US$1; KSh92: £1 (average rates January–August 1997)

**Gross domestic product:** US$9bn (1996)

**GDP shares:** agriculture 30%, tourism 19%, manufacturing 10% (1997)

**GDP per head:** US$285 (1996)

**Average annual rate of inflation:** 11.7% (1984–94); 22.5% (1992–96)

**Source of principal exports:** agriculture (tea, coffee, horticulture); petroleum products

**Main trading partners:** UK, South Africa, Germany, Japan, Uganda, Tanzania

**Foreign debt:** US$7.2bn (1997)

**Debt service ratio:** 20.8% (1997)

**left** Amos Njeli picking passion fruit on his organically farmed plot in Emaloba village, Vihiga

# Sources and further reading

**African Rights:** *Kenya Shadow Justice* (London: African Rights, 1996)

**Simon Baynham:** *Kenya: Prospects for Peace and Stability* (London: Research Institute for the Study of Conflict and Terrorism, *Conflict Studies 297*, 1997)

**Bruce Berman and John Lonsdale:** *Unhappy Valley: Clan, Class and State in Colonial Kenya* (London: James Currey, 1992)

**Human Rights Watch/Africa Watch:** *Divide and Rule: State-Sponsored Ethnic Violence in Kenya* (New York and London: Human Rights Watch, 1997)

**Calestous Juma and J. B. Ojwang (eds):** *In Land We Trust: Environment, Private Property, and Constitutional Change* (London: Zed, 1996)

**Greet Kershaw:** *Mau Mau from Below* (Oxford: James Currey, 1997)

**Fiona Mackenzie:** *Land, Ecology and Resistance in Kenya* (Edinburgh: Edinburgh University Press, 1997)

**George Monbiot:** *No Man's Land: An Investigative Journey through Kenya and Tanzania* (London: Picador, 1994)

**L. Ng'ang'a, J. Ngugi and G. Williams:** *Youth-to-Youth: HIV Prevention and Young People in Kenya* (Nairobi: Kenya AIDS NGOs Consortium)

**Ngugi wa Thiong'o:** *Detained: A Writer's Prison Diary* (London: Heinemann)

**Ngugi wa Thiong'o:** *Moving the Centre: The Struggle for Cultural Freedom* (London: James Currey, 1993)

**William R. Ochieng' (ed):** *Themes in Kenyan History* (London: James Currey, 1991)

**B.A. Ogot and W.R. Ochieng' (eds):** *Decolonization and Independence in Kenya 1940–93* (London: James Currey, 1995)

**Thomas Spear and Richard Waller:** *Being Maasai: Ethnicity and Identity in East Africa* (London: James Currey, 1993)

**Barbara Thomas-Slater:** *Gender, Environment, and Development in Kenya: A Grassroots Perspective* (Boulder: Lynne Rienner, 1995)

**Mary Tiffen, Michael Mortimore, and Francis Gichuki:** *More People, Less Erosion: Environmental Recovery in Kenya* (London and Chichester: ODI and John Wiley, 1994)

**Richard Trillo:** *Kenya: The Rough Guide* (London: Rough Guides, 1996)

**below** A mobile school in Dambas, Wajir District: children with their *loh*, the wooden boards from which they learn the verses of the Koran

# Acknowledgements

My greatest thanks must go to all the Kenyans, from every corner of the country, who have never failed to make me feel welcome. They have enriched my life.

This book also depends heavily on contributions by Robin Palmer, Adam Leach, and George Monbiot; and on the support of Karen Twining, Ian Leggett, and all of Oxfam's staff in Kenya.

Lastly I want to thank the drivers, Peter Thuo and Robert Ngugi, for their companionship and ideas.

*Asanteni sana.*

Geoff Sayer

**right** Wajir Town: Araba Derow experiments with the author's camera

# Oxfam in Kenya

Some of the individuals and communities featured in this book receive support from Oxfam GB. Oxfam has been associated with Kenya since Independence and has worked there for over 15 years. During major droughts in the early 1980s, emergency relief programmes were established in northern Kenya, providing humanitarian assistance to thousands of people in pastoralist areas.

Working with local organisations and through its own activities, Oxfam is helping poor people in rural communities to acquire practical skills and so become self-sufficient. Poor households in farming communities are encouraged to adopt low-cost and environmentally sound agricultural methods to improve food production. Nomadic pastoralist communities are helped to get access to veterinary services and water sources for their livestock. Practical support is also given to community health activities, and the improvement of rural water supplies, with a special focus on the needs of women. Several organisations receive support to create outlets for products that are traded fairly and earn a decent income for the producers.

The long-term security of people's livelihoods depends partly on support from government and other institutions, so Oxfam has helped poor communities to acquire organisational skills and take advantage of opportunities to represent their needs.

Oxfam continues to work closely with local communities and government to provide food relief in response to droughts and other disasters in arid areas. Emergency assistance is provided in ways that ensure that supplies of food and other items are distributed fairly, in a manner that is accountable to local people.

Since the early 1990s, Oxfam has helped displaced people to rehabilitate themselves following the political instability and ethnic conflict which have affected large numbers of people throughout Kenya. Oxfam and other organisations have provided them with household materials, agricultural equipment, and practical advice on food production and income generation. Oxfam also supports practical work to resolve conflict and help local leaders to restore peace between pastoral communities, both within Kenya and across the border with Uganda.

In urban areas of Kenya, some of the worst consequences of poverty are felt most acutely by women and children. Oxfam funds a range of projects which provide practical support to very young children employed as domestic workers in Nairobi; training and education on the rights of girl children is offered to local groups, and support for women's small-scale businesses. Oxfam supports organisations which provide legal advice and assistance to help poor people find shelter in low-income urban areas.

There is a growing awareness about the nature and causes of poverty in Kenya. With Oxfam's help, local organisations are taking action to tackle the vulnerability and destitution of very poor people. Women's groups are working to increase awareness of the nature and level of violence against women, and to promote ways of challenging it. Action is also being taken by local communities and by Oxfam and other agencies to improve security of land tenure, especially in urban slums; to help ensure national food security; and to represent the needs of poor pastoralist communities.

**left** A community paravet prepares to treat a camel with oxytetracyclin antibiotic in Wajir District, where Oxfam has supported the development of Pastoral Associations

71